designer
SOAPMAKING

designer
SOAPMAKING

Marie Browning

Sterling Publishing Co., Inc.
New York

Prolific Impressions Production Staff:

Editor in Chief: Mickey Baskett
Copy Editor: Phyllis Mueller
Graphics: Dianne Miller, Karen Turpin
Styling: Kirsten Jones
Photography: Jerry Mucklow
Administration: Jim Baskett

Library of Congress Cataloging-in-Publication Data Available

10 9 8 7 6 5 4 3 2 1

Published by Sterling Publishing Co., Inc.
387 Park Avenue South, New York, N.Y. 10016

© 2003 by Prolific Impressions, Inc.

Produced by Prolific Impressions, Inc.
160 South Candler St., Decatur, GA 30030

Distributed in Canada by Sterling Publishing
c/o Canadian Manda Group, One Atlantic Avenue, Suite 105
Toronto, Ontario, Canada M6K 3E7
Distributed in Great Britain by Chrysalis Books
64 Brewery Road, London N7 9NT, England
Distributed in Australia by Capricorn Link (Australia) Pty. Ltd.
P.O. Box 704, Windsor, NSW 2756 Australia

Printed in China
Sterling ISBN 1-4027-0342-2

Acknowledgments

Marie Browning would like to thank the following companies for their generous contributions of product:

Aquarius Aromatherapy & Soap
Mission, BC, Canada
www.aquariusaroma-soap.com
On-line suppliers of melt and pour soap bases, molds, fragrances, colorants, additives, inclusions, oils, packaging, and information on all aspects of soapmaking.

Delta Technical Coatings
Whittier, CA, USA
www.deltacrafts.com
Manufacturers of Soap Creations line of melt and pour soap bases, molds, fragrances, cosmetic glitters, and colorants.

Environmental Technology, Inc.
Fields Landing, CA, USA
www.eti-usa.com
Manufacturers of Fields Landing Soap Factory line of melt and pour soap bases, including true coconut oil soap base, plastic tube molds, tray molds, resin molds, fragrances, colorants, and soap kits.

Image Hill
North Kansas City, MO, USA
www.soapexpressions.com
Manufacturers of Soap Expressions line of melt and pour soap bases, tray molds, metal tube molds, fragrances, colorants, additives, and soap kits.

Life of the Party
North Brunswick, NJ, USA
www.soapplace.com
Manufacturers of melt and pour soap bases, molds, fragrances, colorants, additives, and soap kits.

Martin Creative
Black Creek, BC, Canada
www.martincreative.com
High quality designer soap molds, including two-part plastic tube molds.

Continued on next page

Milky Way Molds
Portland, OR, USA
www.milkywaymolds.com
High quality designer soap molds, soap stamps, and two-part plastic tube molds.

TKB Trading
Oakland, CA, USA
www.tkbtrading.com
On-line suppliers of melt and pour soap bases, vegetable soap bases for hand milling, molds, fragrances, colorants, additives, inclusions, oils, and information on all aspects of soapmaking. TKB also manufactures high-quality soap colorants.

Yaley Enterprises
Redding, CA, USA
www.yaley.com
Manufacturers of Soapsations™ line of melt and pour soap bases, molds, candle molds, fragrances, and colorants.

MARIE
BROWNING

About the Author

Marie Browning is a consummate craft designer who has made a career of designing products, writing books and articles, and teaching and demonstrating. You may have been charmed by her creative acumen but not been aware of the woman behind it; she has designed stencils, stamps, transfers, and a variety of other products for art and craft supply companies.

This book is her fourth book about soapmaking. The others are *300 Soap Recipes* (Sterling, 2002), *Natural Soapmaking* (Sterling, 1998), and *Melt & Pour Soapmaking* (Sterling, 2000). In addition to books about soapmaking, Browning has authored three other books published by Sterling: *Handcrafted Journals, Albums, Scrapbooks & More* (1999); *Making Glorious Gifts from Your Garden* (1999); *Crafting with Vellum and Parchment*; *Hand Decorating*

Paper; and *Family Photocrafts* (2000). Her articles and designs have appeared in *Handcraft Illustrated, Better Homes & Gardens, Canadian Stamper, Great American Crafts, All American Crafts,* and in numerous project books published by Plaid Enterprises, Inc.

Marie Browning earned a Fine Arts Diploma from Camosun College and attended the University of Victoria. She is a Certified Professional Demonstrator, a professional affiliate of the Canadian Craft and Hobby Association, and a member of the Stencil Artisans League and the Society of Craft Designers.

She lives, gardens, and crafts on Vancouver Island in Canada. She and her husband Scott have three children: Katelyn, Lena, and Jonathan.

Visit Marie at www.mariebrowning.com. ❑

6

This book shows you, step-by-step, how to make an assortment of gorgeous, colorful, fragrant soaps that you'll love creating, using, and giving. It's easy and fun to do when you use melt and pour soap bases and the variety of molds and tools available in stores and through mail order.

You'll learn techniques for making picture soaps, both tube molded and loaf

You Can Make Designer Soaps At Home!

style, embedded soaps, and embossed soaps, including a new custom embossing method that uses polymer clay motifs you can make at home. Instructions for making fossil soaps, which are fun to create with and give to children, and carving simple designs in soaps are included. You'll also learn creative techniques for packaging and displaying your soap creations.

There are numerous photographs to guide you, and recipes and patterns are provided. Have fun being a soap designer!

Marie Browning

7

Contents

Soapmaking has never been easier or more creative. There are ready-made soap bases available that just need to be melted and molded. Essential oils and soap-making scents add to the pleasure and sensory results of the soapmaking process.

Soapmaking Supplies

Intermixable colorants make it easy to create the colors of your choice. And molds of all types make it easy to be creative.

The soaps in this book are intended to be made with melt and pour soap bases and will not be as successful with cold process or handmilled soapmaking techniques. In this section, you'll learn about the variety of soapmaking supplies available.

SOAP BASES

■ Melt and Pour Soap Bases

Easy to use melt and pour soap bases have taken the mystery out of making all kinds of soaps. There are many types of melt and pour soap bases, and they vary in quality. The three basic soap bases are clear glycerin soap base, whitened glycerin soap base, and white coconut oil soap base. All are available at crafts stores. (You can't use bars of glycerin soap from the bath products section – they will not melt!)

Variations of the three bases involve the addition of additives such as olive oil, coconut oil, hemp oil, or colorants. They all are designed to melt easily in a microwave or a double boiler and be poured into molds.

There are some important differences between melt and pour soaps and handmilled and cold processed soaps:

• Water is **never** added to melt and pour soap bases. It makes them slimy and prevents the soap from hardening properly.

• Melt and pour soaps **set up immediately** with little curing time, enabling you to create handmade soaps almost instantly.

• The **creative and design possibilities are greater** with the melt and pour soap method.

■ White Coconut Oil Soap Base

Coconut oil soap base is true coconut oil soap, not just whitened glycerin soap with added coconut oil. Made with coconut and vegetable oils, this pH balanced soap is enriched with vitamin E. It makes your skin feel soft, clean, and healthy, and the coconut oil creates a protective layer that keeps skin supple.

It is easy to tell if you are working with true coconut oil soap:

• When melted, coconut oil soap is clear; when fully hardened, it turns bright white.

• Coconut oil soap base has a high melting point (190 degrees F.), so it makes for a wonderful hard-finished soap.

• The high melting temperature can also melt some molds, so be sure to cool down the melted soap by stirring before pouring it into a mold.

Clear Glycerin Soap Base

High quality glycerin soap should be gentle enough for all skin types and have very little scent so it is ready for your own fragrant blends. If you wish a cloudy glycerin soap to be more transparent when molded, simply melt it, let it harden, and re-melt before pouring in your mold. Re-melting helps remove excess moisture from the soap. Most glycerin soaps have a melting point of 135-145 degrees F.

Whitened Glycerin Soap Base

Most white melt and pour bases are glycerin soap whitened with titanium dioxide, a powdered pigment. These soap bases may be called coconut oil soap when coconut oil is added. The soap has a milky, translucent look and a lower melting point than white coconut oil soap. When melted, the soap remains milky-looking. You can make your own whitened glycerin soap by simply adding white colorant to clear soap base – this enables you to achieve different effects by adding a little white for a translucent bar or more for an opaque bar.

Other Soap Bases

Other soap bases are glycerin based and have added ingredients that provide different qualities to the soap. Some examples include:

- *Glycerin with added coconut oil* - Opaque white; often has a light coconut scent.
- *Glycerin with added avocado and cucumber* - Opaque, pale green; enriched with vitamin E; has a suspension formula to keep additives uniformly distributed.
- *Glycerin with added olive oil* - Translucent amber or green color; added olive oil hydrates the skin and contains vitamin E and antioxidants; may have a suspension formula.
- *Glycerin with added hemp oil* - Translucent green; silky and soothing; good for dry skin; recognized for its ability to repair damaged skin cells.
- *Glycerin with added goat's milk* - Opaque white; gently moisturizes while maintaining the skin's natural pH.
- *Colored glycerin soap bases* - Include clear colored soap bases, opaque colored soap bases, and bright florescent colored bases.

FRAGRANCE

Adding fragrant oils is a significant part of creating soaps. Although some scent in a soap bar comes from additives, that scent alone is not strong enough to create a beautiful aromatic soap bar.

The two main types of oils are essential oils and fragrance oils. When buying oils for scenting, carry along a bag of freshly ground (unused) coffee and sniff it to help clear your nose. *Do not* use flavored extracts, potpourri oils, or candle scents in your soaps.

Essential Oils

The fresh scents of flowers and herbs are created by oils in the cells of the plants, which are known as essential oils. Of the many thousands of plants in the world, only about 200 produce essential oils used in the art of perfumery. Capturing the fragrance of flowers has been performed since ancient times for fragrance, healing, and mood altering.

Essential oils are highly concentrated and must be diluted before they can be safely applied to the skin or blended into soaps (one percent or less is considered to be a safe level for soapmaking). Too much essential oil can cause severe skin irritations. People with sensitive skin or allergies should be careful when using essential oils in their soap.

Fragrance Oils

Fragrance oils are synthetically produced scents. They are much cheaper to produce than essential oils and, therefore, cost less. Since fragrance oils are not derived from specific plants, they are available in a wider range of scents and blends than essential oils, and many high quality fragrance oils are actually blends of essential oils.

Your nose can play a substantial role in determining the quality of a fragrance oil. Oils cut (diluted) with alcohol tend to smell alike and have a sharp bite to them. Quality, uncut fragrance oils have a smooth, concentrated smell. Fragrance oils with alcohol can adversely affect melt and pour soap bases – the alcohol pushes out the moisture in the soap base, forming white crystals on the soap.

When making soap, you need to use more of a lower quality (cut) fragrance oil than you would of a high quality fragrance oil to achieve the same results. Since less oil is required, and the true smell is often what prompts someone to use a soap, good quality fragrance oils are a wise investment.

Blending Fragrances

The trend today is for single scented perfumes that smell like natural botanicals, such as a freshly sliced orange or a fresh sprig of peppermint. Though these scents smell like the original fruit, flower, or herb, they also contain other scents to make them lasting and more charming. These different notes are broken down into three main elements:

Main scent - The key or main scent in your blend. These are the "high notes" – the first aromas your nose detects.

Blenders - Additional scents to enhance the main scent. They are the "middle notes" of a blend.

Contrasting scents - These scents liven up the blend and provide the "low notes" or long lasting scents.

Here's an example: The **main scent** is the overall aroma you wish to create, such as the floral scent of rose. The **blender scent** could be spicy notes of clove that enhance the main scent. The **contrasting scent** could be vanilla, which livens up the scent without overpowering the top two scents and provides the lasting note.

Continued on next page

SCENT GROUPS

Following is a partial list of fragrances and the scent groups to which they belong:

Citrus
Grapefruit • Lemon
Lime • Mandarin
Pink Grapefruit • Sweet orange
Tangerine

Spicy
Cinnamon • Clove
Ginger • Vanilla

Herbal
Chamomile • Cucumber
Eucalyptus • Juniper
Peppermint • Pine
Rosemary • Sage
Tea tree

Fruity
Blueberry • Coconut
Green apple • Kiwi
Mango • Melon
Mulberry • Pear

Floral
Jasmine • Lavender
Lilac • Lily of the valley
Plumaria • Rose
Violet • Ylang-ylang

Earthy
Amber • Frankincense
Honey • Musk
Patchouli • Sandalwood

Blended Fragrances
Baby powder • Brown sugar
Candy cane • Chocolate
Honey almond • Ocean
Rain • Sunflower

Scent Substitutions

If you cannot find the fragrance listed for the recipe, simply substitute another fragrance or fragrance blend. Some substitute scents are obvious, such as using sweet orange or tangerine for Orange Slice soap. For others scents, such as the pine and rain blend for the Fore! soap, you could substitute any fresh, outdoors-y scent blend such as sandalwood and juniper. Experiment with your own scent blends to become your own soap designer.

Aromatherapy

Aromatherapy is rooted in herbal medicine that dates back to prehistoric times. The ancient Egyptians, Greeks, Romans, and Hebrews all documented the use of fragrances for cosmetic and medicinal purposes. Today, leading cosmetic firms have introduced an aromatherapy line that presents the beneficial aspects of fragrances.

It is the essential oils of a plant, sometimes dubbed the plant's "soul" or "spirit," that are believed to affect our emotional, physical, and aesthetic well-being. While no medical claims can be made, it is certainly no surprise that a relaxing, scented bath can soothe us and renew our spirit.

Many essential oils have specific effects and qualities attributed to them. Below is a brief list of the most basic applications:

- **Peaceful and relaxing** - Lavender, sandalwood, honeysuckle, chamomile, ylang-ylang, tangerine, rose, lemon verbena

POINTS TO CONSIDER WHEN CREATING BLENDS

- A fixative takes the place of the plant's cells and holds the scent. The fixative can be unscented or add its own aroma to the blend. In soap crafting, the fixative can be the soap base or dried botanical additives. The fixative is necessary to give the blend a long-lasting quality and release the fragrance moderately over time.

- Test your fragrant blends by placing a few drops of oil on a paper towel. Let the fragrance oils blend for a few hours, then sniff the blend to evaluate.

- Some people enjoy the rich, exotic smell of warm and earthy scents; others love the refreshing, clean aromas of citrus or herbal and fresh scent categories. You will naturally choose scents that appeal to you.

- These scents are considered natural blenders because they mix well with scents from other scent categories: lime, peppermint, lavender, rose, jasmine, sandalwood, vanilla, cinnamon, and honey.

- Dry skin does not hold fragrance as well as skin that is well hydrated.

- **Energizing** - Rosemary, peppermint, lemon, lime, jasmine, honey

- **Stimulating and uplifting** - Bergamot, orange, jasmine, rosemary, lemon verbena, mints, sage, pine

- **Antiseptic** - tea tree, eucalyptus, peppermint, lavender

- **Focusing, head-clearing** - Frankincense, peppermint, grapefruit, cinnamon, chamomile, lavender, orange, ylang-ylang

Scientific research is not conclusive about whether the benefits of aromatherapy are the result of the aroma or of other properties of essential oils. I use both essential oils and synthetic fragrance oils in my soap recipes.

COLORANTS

Color is another important part of soap's allure. You can add spices and dried herbs for an earthy-looking soap or cosmetic grade colorants for a brightly colored bar.

Liquids

Cosmetic grade colorants in liquid form can be found in the fragrance-crafting department of your local craft store or from soapmaking suppliers. High quality cosmetic grade colorants create true, clean colors and are excellent for blending and creating many different hues. Liquid colors come in red, blue, yellow, orange, green, white, and black. Food coloring is **not** suitable for soapmaking, as the color quickly fades.

Solid Colorants

Soap colorants in solid form also are available in a wide selection of mixed hues and can be found at many craft supply stores or departments.

Glitter Colorants

For a sparkling effect, cosmetic grade glitters are available. These are superfine and are not abrasive to the skin.

Continued on next page

17

■ Natural Color Agents

Soaps colored with natural powders have a natural, country look with attractive warm brown and tan hues. Many additives impart interesting colors and textures to your soap. Some natural powders include cocoa powder, dried herbs, and ground spices.

■ Color Mixing Basics

The best way to learn about color mixing is through personal experience and experimentation. To get started, it helps to understand a few basic principles.

Primary colors are red, blue, and yellow. *Secondary colors* are mixes of primary colors – green (yellow + blue), purple (red + blue), and orange (red + yellow). *Intermediate colors* are mixes of a primary color with a neighboring secondary color; e.g., lime green, which is a mixture of yellow + green.

Complementary colors are colors that are opposite one another on the color wheel – red is the complement of green, purple is the complement of yellow, blue is the complement of orange. When you mix a color with its complement; the result is a dulling or muting of the color, making it less intense. Here are some examples:

- Dusty plum - Purple + a touch of its complement, yellow
- Golden ocher - Yellow + a touch of its complement, purple

Shades are made by adding black to a color. *Tints* are made by adding white.

CONSIDERATIONS FOR COLORANTS

- Because results can vary a great deal depending on the size or number of drops you use, take notes while mixing colors and keep a record of your results.

- The soap base used affects the color of the finished soap. In a clear base, colors appear clear and jewel-toned; in a white base, they look softer and pastel-colored.

- Some colorants are transparent and leave glycerin soap bases clear, while others add an opaque tint. To avoid disappointment, test your colorants in a small amount of the base before making a large batch.

- Some fragrance oils are strongly colored and will influence the color of your soap. Adding a fragrance oil such as vanilla, which has a strong amber hue, to a clear blue soap will give the soap a greenish tint.

- Adding too much colorant makes the color migrate through the soap faster. For example, if you are making a two-colored soap of white and red; the deeply colored red section of the soap design may bleed into the white section of the soap over time.

ADDITIVES

Additives like oatmeal, dried herbs, and extra oils can be added to soap bases to nourish, soften, and provide gentle scrubbing properties. Additives used in the soap recipes in this book can be found at grocery stores, health food stores, and craft supply outlets. Each ingredient offers unique characteristics to your products. In this book, additives are used mainly for their color and visual appeal.

Remember these points when you are including additives in your soaps:

- Always use recommended, safe ingredients. Just because an ingredient is natural, it doesn't mean it is safe to use in your soap.

- Too much of an additive may soften your soap or make it scratchy and uncomfortable to use. For best results, follow the recipe and use the recommended amount.

- Measure additives and blend well before adding them to melted soap. Additives such as powdered milks and spices can clump up – mixing them with liquid glycerin before stirring into melted soap helps disperse additives evenly.

- Additives such as powdered spices, seeds, or grains will either sink or float, giving the soap a natural, whimsical look. To achieve this effect, add the additives to the melted soap base before pouring or place them in the bottom of the mold before pouring the melted soap.

- To suspend additives throughout the soap, you need to do an extra step. After adding the additives to the melted soap, gently stir the soap with a spoon to slowly cool and thicken it. Immediately after the soap starts to thicken, pour the soap in the mold. The soap will harden with the additives suspended throughout the soap. Be careful not to let the soap thicken so much that it becomes too thick to pour. If this happens, simply re-melt and start again. Some soap bases are specially formulated to suspend additives. When you use them you need only add the additives, mix, and pour in the mold.

- Don't use fresh organic materials such as vegetables and fruits in melt and pour soap bases. A material that is not properly dried or preserved can cause your soap to quickly become rancid.

- Beware of soap recipes that seem impractical or for looks only. For example, commercial potpourri may look good sprinkled in a clear soap, but the large petals will clog your drain and scratch your skin. Commercial potpourri also may contain ingredients that would be extremely dangerous to your skin.

- When adding extra oils, add a natural preservative for a longer lasting bar. Natural preservatives include citric acid, vitamin E oil, and grapefruit seed extract.

Safe Additives for Soaps

Dried Botanicals (NOT Fresh)
Crushed apricot seed
Eucalyptus leaves • Green tea
Lavender buds • Lemon peel
Lemon verbena leaves
Lemongrass • Loofah
Orange peel • Peppermint leaves
Poppy seeds • Rose petals
Rosehip powder • Rosemary leaves
Sage leaves • Sandalwood

Nuts
Almond • Coconut • Hazelnut

Oils
Sweet almond oil • Coconut oil
Cocoa butter • Olive oil
Palm oil • Shea nut butter

Spices
Allspice • Anise
Cardamom • Cinnamon
Clove • Paprika (use sparingly)
Tumeric • Vanilla pod (seeds)

Miscellaneous
Aloe vera gel • Cornmeal
Glycerin (liquid) • Honey
Milk (powdered whole milk, goat's milk, and buttermilk)
Oatmeal • Ground pumice
Tapioca • Wheat bran

Preservatives
Citric acid • Grapefruit seed extract
Vitamin E oil (break open a capsule and squirt the oil into melted soap)

MOLDS

Molds help your melt and pour soaps look professional and fancy. Most designs in this book use easy to find tray molds, loaf molds, and tube molds. I also used plastic containers, plastic straws, and pieces of PVC pipe as molds.

Most soap molds can tolerate temperatures of 135-145 degrees F. Over-heated soap can sometimes warp even the best soap molds – this is more likely with coconut oil soap, which has a higher melting point (190 degrees F.). For high-temperature pours, cool the soap by stirring or place the molds in a shallow pan of cold water.

Molded designs show up clearer and crisper in hard soap than in soft soap. Adding palm oil or cocoa butter can harden softer glycerin soaps; adding these oils clouds clear glycerin soap.

Pictured right: Novelty shapes in trays are available in craft departments and can be used for soap-making and candle-making.

Pictured below: Food storage containers of flexible plastic make great molds.

Pictured on next page: A variety of molds that are especially made for soap-making and candle-making. Shown are tube molds in plastic, metal, PVC, and two-part clear plastic. Shown also are two individual shaped molds used for resin casting that serve just as well for soap-making.

Tube Molds

Tube molds are available in plastic and metal, in both tubular and two-part snap-together styles. Having a selection of large and small molds in basic shapes enables you to make a wide selection of designs. The plastic tube molds created for soapmaking create beautiful bars of soap and have other crafting and culinary uses. Metal molds should be used with a mold release.

Metal candle molds can handle high temperatures; however, most soap naturally reacts with metal, especially aluminum. This reaction causes the metal to corrode quickly, which in turn discolors your soap, and this corrosion can eventually destroy metal molds.

Some plastic candle molds are suitable for soap crafting. Because they are designed to withstand the high temperatures of melted wax, they can hold hot soap without melting. To make it easier to remove the soap, choose low and wide molds rather than long and skinny ones and always use a mold release.

PVC Molds

You can create your own round tube molds using plastic PVC plumbing pipe from the hardware store. The pipe is inexpensive and comes in a variety of diameters. To make a mold, use a hacksaw to cut the pipe into 6" lengths. Sand all the cut edges smooth before using, and follow the tube mold preparation directions before pouring in the melted soap.

Loaf Molds

Loaf molds come in small, medium, and large sizes and allow you to pour many bars at once. I prefer large loaf-style tube molds because you can pour two or three bars to test a design before producing a large quantity.

Novelty Molds & Trays

Molds made for soapmaking come in individual shapes or in a tray of fancy motifs and are designed to last a long time. They can withstand the high temperature of melt and pour soap bases without warping or melting. Look for quality soap molds that don't require pre-treatment to release the hardened soaps and are designed to be self-leveling. Small shape molds are great for chunk style soaps. Look for them at crafts stores.

Individual resin casting molds are an excellent size and depth for single bars of homemade soap. The number of ounces of melted soap the mold holds is printed on the bottom of each mold.

Candy & Plaster Molds

Molds made for plaster and candy can warp and melt from the high temperatures of melted soap, spilling their contents and causing burns. You can, however, use these molds if you carefully follow these steps:

1. Pour 1" of water in a shallow pan and place in the freezer.

2. When the water has frozen solid, remove the pan from the freezer to your work area.

3. Place the mold on the ice and let sit a few minutes until cold.

4. Pour the melted soap in the mold and let harden.

5. Wipe the moisture off the bottom of the mold and release the molded soap.

Note: After a candy mold has been used for soapmaking, it can't be used for making candy.

Plastic Food Storage Containers

Small sandwich or small plastic storage containers can accommodate loaf style soap recipes. Try to find ones with no design on the inside bottom and with rounded corners.

Be careful when choosing plastic containers for molding your soaps. Some cannot withstand the high temperature of melted soap and will melt and collapse, spilling the hot soap. Choose containers that are dishwasher safe and avoid disposable plastic containers and takeout food containers. Always stir the soap before pouring to help cool it.

Continued on next page

Many plastic containers designed to keep food from crushing are tempting to use because of their wonderful designs and deep shapes, but the plastic will warp and melt when soap is added. Most plastic cups are unsuitable for soapmaking molds.

Releasing Soap from Molds

• Release soap from tray molds by using gentle thumb pressure on the back of the mold. You can easily damage molds with improper handling.

• To help soap release from the mold, I prefer petroleum jelly. It is widely used in cosmetics as an emollient and barrier cream. I found it an excellent mold conditioner and release. It doesn't leave a sticky residue on the soap.

• A homemade soap release comes from the manufacturer of Milky Way soap molds: Melt one part paraffin wax (by weight). Stir in 3 parts baby oil. Best used when hot, the mixture can be applied when cold as a soft paste. Make sure you have thin and even application; otherwise, it can mar the smoothness of the finished soap.

• Vegetable oil in liquid and spray form is also used as a mold release, but I don't recommend it. Even a thin film on the mold tends to make the soap a bit greasy, and the oil can become rancid over time, altering the fragrance of the soap.

• Soap that remains in a mold for 12-24 hours after cooling is much easier to release than soap that is unmolded immediately upon cooling.

• If you can't get your soap to release from a mold, try placing the mold in the freezer for 10 minutes. Then try to release.

Capacity of Soap Molds

Most of the time I measure by eye and melt more soap base than I think I'll need, since the leftover melted soap is great for small soap projects and I know I can always re-melt it for future projects. I pour any leftover soap base in small plastic containers and keep the colors separated.

Below, I've provided some examples of how I calculate the soap required for each recipe. I recommend you start with smaller batches to get used to the process before you make larger batches. Remember – if a batch doesn't look as you expected, it can still be used.

I have include the capacity of a number of molds here. However, to calculate the amount of soap needed to fill other molds you own, fill the mold with water and pour the water in a measuring cup. Melt an additional 1 oz. of soap base to allow for the soap that clings to the sides of the measuring cup.

Calculating How Much Soap Base to Melt

Tube Molds

Here's how I calculate how much melted soap I need for a tube-molded design bar. I'm using the Fish Bowl Soap as an example.

Molds & Capacities:
One medium circle tube mold, 12 oz. capacity
One 4" long small heart tube (fish) = 4 oz.
Two 4" long small circle tubes (large bubbles) = 2 oz.
Soap to fill straw holes (small bubbles and eye in fish) =
    1 oz.

Calculation:
Place fish and bubble pieces in medium circle tube mold. Melted soap required to fill mold = 5 oz. (Subtract 4 oz. (fish) + 2 oz. (bubbles) + 1 oz. (bubbles) from 12 oz. (capacity of mold).) The finished loaf of soap makes four 1" slices of soap, 3 oz. each.

Continued on next page

Continued from page 23

Loaf Molds

And here's how I calculate the melted soap required for a loaf mold design bar. I'm using the Star Flowers recipe, which makes four bars, as an example.

Molds & Capacities:

Loaf mold, 16 oz. capacity

Two 4" pieces in small star tube (star flowers) = 8 oz.

Four 4" pieces cut from one small star tube (leaves) = 4 oz.

Calculation:

Place star flowers and leaf pieces in small loaf mold. Melted soap required to fill loaf mold = 4 oz. (Subtract 8 oz. (star flowers) + 4 oz. (leaves) from 16 oz. (capacity of mold).) The finished loaf makes four 1" slices, 4 oz. each.

Capacities of Shape Molds

Following are the capacities (in ounces) of the basic shape molds used in this book.

Mini rectangle (1-1/2" x 1" x 1" deep) = 2 oz.

Small rectangle (2-3/4" x 2" x 1" deep) = 3 oz.

Medium rectangle (3-1/4" x 2-1/4" x 1" deep) = 4 oz.

Medium square (3" x 3" x 1" deep) = 5 oz.

Large rectangle (3" x 6" x 1" deep) = 9 oz.

Medium circle (2-1/2" diameter x 1" deep) = 2-1/2 oz.

Domed small circle (2-1/2" diameter x 3/4" deep) = 2 oz.

Domed medium circle (3" diameter x 1" deep) = 4 oz.

Medium oval (2" x 3" x 3/4" deep) = 2-1/2 oz.

Domed medium oval (3-3/4" x 2-1/2" x 1-1/4" deep) = 4 oz.

Capacities of Loaf Molds

Small loaf mold (3-1/4" x 4-3/4" x 2-1/2" deep food storage container) - 16 oz. to fill

Medium loaf mold (4" x 6" x 2-3/4" deep food storage container) - 24 oz. to fill

Capacities of Tube Molds

This chart lists how much soap is needed to fill 1" of a tube mold. Use it to calculate how much soap base you need for the number of bars you wish to make. My estimates are for 1" thick bars for molds 2-1/2" in diameter or larger and 1/2" thick bars for smaller tubes.

Plastic tube molds made for soap are 6" high; metal tube molds are 9" high. Plastic and metal candle molds range from 4" to 10" in height. The tube mold measurements are taken across the top of the mold and include the width of the mold material.

1" (small) circle - 1/2 oz. per 1"

2" (medium) circle - 1-1/2 oz. per 1"

2-3/4" (medium) circle - 3 oz. per 1"

3-1/2" (large) circle - 5 oz. per 1"

2" x 2-1/2" (medium) oval - 2-1/2 oz. per 1"

2-1/2" x 3-1/2" (large) oval - 4 oz. per 1"

1-1/2" (small) heart - 1 oz. per 1"

3" (large) heart - 4 oz. per 1"

1-1/2" (small) star - 1 oz. per 1"

3" (large) star - 4 oz. per 1"

1-1/2" (small) blossom - 1 oz. per 1"

3" (large) blossom - 3-1/2 oz. per 1"

2-1/2" butterfly - 3-1/2 oz. per 1"

3" hexagon - 4 oz. per 1"

3" x 4" (large) rectangle - 8 oz. per 1"

EQUIPMENT

The basic tools and equipment for creating melt and pour soaps are standard kitchen items that you possibly already own. After using them for soapmaking, if you clean glass and metal tools thoroughly, they can be returned to the kitchen for food preparation. Once used for soapmaking, plastic and wooden items can be used **only** for soapmaking.

Glass measuring cups - 1 cup, 2 cup, and 4 cup heat-resistant measuring cups are the main containers for melting soap bases in the microwave or for the stovetop double boiler method.

Measuring spoons - A set of good metal or plastic measuring spoons are used for measuring additives.

Mixing spoons - Metal or wooden kitchen spoons are needed for mixing melted soap. Metal spoons will not transfer fragrances, so they are safe for food use when you're not using them for soapmaking. If you use wooden spoons, clearly mark them FRAGRANCE CRAFTING ONLY – the wood retains the scents and will transfer them to your cooking.

Wooden craft sticks are also useful for stirring melted soap.

Glass droppers - You will need about 3 glass droppers for measuring fragrance oils. **Do not** use plastic droppers – some essential oils will eat right through them, and because you can't wash out the scents, you could end up contaminating your oils with other scents.

Large saucepan *(for the stovetop method)* - Use a large saucepan – any metal is fine – to hold water and a large heat-resistant glass measuring cup to make a double boiler for melting melt and pour soap bases.

Soap Cutter

Sharp knives - Knives are used to cut soap bases into smaller pieces and to slice finished molded soaps. A variety of sizes, from small paring knives to large butcher knives, is handy.

Soap Beveler

Wax paper - Use wax paper to protect your work area when pouring and creating soaps.

Plastic wrap - Use a good quality cling-style wrap for preparing tube molds and for packaging soap. Use **rubber bands** to hold plastic wrap snugly to tube molds.

Chopsticks - Chopsticks are great for arranging soap pieces in tube molds for picture soaps. I especially like the white plastic chopsticks.

Wooden dowel - A 6" length of a 3/4" diameter wooden dowel is a perfect tool for pushing soap out of small tube molds.

Soap beveler - A soap beveler is really a cheese plane that is used to bevel the soap edges. It can also be used as a planer to clean soap surfaces and make decorative soap curls.

Garnishing tools - Many specialty kitchen tools come in handy for special effects; for example, a garnish cutter slices soap with a decorative wavy cut.

Soap cutter - A soap cutter is a slicing tool with a wavy blade. It's used like a knife and gives a decorative look to soaps.

Paper cups - Small paper cups are handy for pre-measuring additives and to use as equal-size risers for tray molds that won't sit level.

This section contains basic instructions and numerous photographs that show how to make soaps using melt and pour soap bases. You'll also see how to prepare molds, arrange soap pieces for picture soaps, and remove soap from molds after it has hardened.

The soap recipes presented make one to

Techniques

four bars. To make a larger amount of soap, in most cases you can simply double the recipe. For calculating amounts for filling different sizes of molds, refer to the previous sections on mold capacities.

As you become familiar with the techniques and procedures, feel free to experiment and come up with your own original signature soaps. Enjoy being your own soap designer!

BASIC STEPS
for Melt & Pour Soapmaking

Photo 1 - Cut the soap base into pieces.

1. Cut up the soap base into small pieces for quick, easy melting. (photo 1) Be sure all bowls, measuring cups, and mixing spoons are completely dry. **Never** add water to melt and pour bases.

2. Place the soap in a heat-resistant measuring cup. (photo 2)

3. Microwave 30 seconds to 1 minute on high for approximately 1 cup of soap pieces. (photo 3) The melting time varies depending on the amount of soap and the type of soap. Melting the soap in brief intervals will keep it from boiling over.

   Option: Melt the soap in a double boiler on the stove. Adjust the heat to keep the soap at a constant liquid point.

   • **Do not** leave soap heating for more than 10 minutes.

   • **Do not** leave a mixing spoon in the soap while heating in the microwave or melting on the stovetop.

4. Remove from the microwave and stir lightly to completely melt the remaining soap pieces and cool down the soap. (photo 4)

Photo 2 - Place the pieces in a heat-resistant glass measuring cup.

Photo 3 - Put the measuring cup in the microwave.

28

- It is harmless to re-melt the soap.

- Always have an extra mold on hand when you are creating your soaps. If you melt more soap than fills your chosen mold, pour the leftover soap in another mold or a plastic container. Let cool, release, and re-melt for another project. Repeated re-melting of clear glycerin soap base makes it more transparent; repeated re-melting of coconut oil soap base makes a harder bar of soap.

- When cleaning up, **don't** put measuring cups or spoons in the dishwasher. Soap left on the equipment could foam and cause the dishwasher to leak. Roll up your sleeves and wash the few pieces of equipment by hand.

Photo 4 - Stir the melting soap.

5. Immediately add additives and/or colorants to the melted soap. (photo 5) Stir in gently to mix. Add the drops of fragrance oil until desired level of fragrance is achieved. If the soap starts to solidify, gently reheat to re-melt it.

6. Pour the soap in the mold. (photo 6)

7. Let the soap cool and harden completely before removing from the mold. The soap will pop out easily when completely set. (photo 7) For a fast set, place the soap in the refrigerator until cool.

Photo 5 - Add colorant.

Photo 6 - Pour the melted, colored, scented soap in the mold.

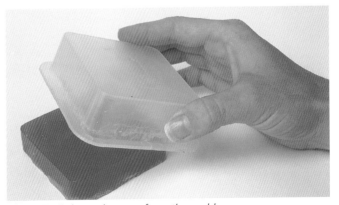

Photo 7 - Release the soap from the mold.

The basic picture soap technique involves placing smaller soap pieces in larger molds to create a variety of design "pictures" that last the life of the soap. Designs can be as simple as a small star in a larger star or a more complicated composition, such as the Martini soap. Picture soaps can be made in tube molds,

Picture Soaps

in loaf style molds, or even in bar shape molds that make only one bar at a time.

This section will also introduce more basic soapmaking techniques such as mold preparation, unmolding your soaps and slicing them. The design possiblilities become endless with each project.

BASIC TECHNIQUES FOR SUCCESS

■ Mold Preparation

1. Prepare both plastic or metal molds by coating the inside of the mold with a thin layer of petroleum jelly to aid in releasing the soap.

2. When using a tube mold, place four layers of plastic wrap over the bottom of the tube mold and attach with a rubber band (photo 1) *or* put on the cap if the mold came with one.

3. You must pour a soap plug each and every time you make soap in a tube mold. Failing to prepare the mold with a plug, even if the mold has a cap, will result in soap seeping out of the mold and all over your work area. To make the plug, pour 1/2" of melted soap to create a seal at the base of the mold. (photo 2) Let harden.

4. Place the prepared mold in a small plastic container. This ensures that if your mold does leak, the soap will be safely contained and can easily be re-melted for future use. You will also be able to move the mold after pouring the soap. Now you're ready to pour.

An easy way to start making your picture soaps is to use an individual bar mold for the final molding. Small pieces of hardened or pre-molded soap are cut and fit into the mold. Melted soap is poured into the mold to create just a single bar of soap.

When using tube molds to make the picture soaps, long "columns" or pre-molded soap shapes are placed into large diameter tube molds. Melted soap is poured around these pre-molded columns and allowed to harden. When the mold is released, it is sliced – and the result is a picture in each slice. Tube molds come in many different styles, designs, and sizes. Small, medium, and large molds make for endless design possibilities! Most of the picture soaps I make are done with this technique.

Loaf style molds can also be used for the final molding, but the technique of placing the pieces is slightly different than if using tube molds. When using a tube mold, you will be placing the smaller columns into the tubes and looking straight down into the picture you are creating. When using a loaf mold for the final molding, the individual columns that make the picture pieces are "stacked" into the loaf mold, which makes it harder for you to see the picture and arrange the pieces.

One advantage a vertical tube mold has over a horizontal loaf mold is that you can pour only an inch or two of soap rather than filling the entire mold. This is a great way to use small bits of soap and make small batches.

Photo 1 - Prepare tube mold with plastic wrap over the bottom.

Photo 2 - Pour the plug.

Creating Dots in Soap

This technique is great for making seeds in the Watermelon Slice soap or the details in the Strawberry Heart soap.

1. When the soap plug has hardened, push in plastic straws.

2. Pour melted soap in the mold around the straws. (photo 3) Let harden completely.

3. Remove the straws without releasing the soap from the mold. If you have trouble removing a straw, grasp it with a pair of pliers, twist, and pull. This will result in holes being left in the soap.

4. Fill the holes with another color of melted soap.(photo 4) Let harden.

Photo 3 - Pour soap in the mold around the straws.

Photo 4 - Remove the straws and fill the holes left by straws with a different color soap base.

Arranging Soap Pieces in Larger Molds

To make picture soaps, smaller molded soap pieces are arranged in a larger mold. (photo 5) Then a contrasting color of soap base is added to fill the space in around the arranged pieces. Here are some tips for creating designs in soaps:

• **Use chopsticks.** When arranging small soap pieces in large tube molds, a pair of chopsticks is handy for moving the pieces around.

• **Chill the pieces.** The smaller the soap columns you place in a large mold, the greater the chance of the pieces melting when you pour hot soap around them. Place the smaller soap pieces in the refrigerator for about 10 minutes to chill them before placing them in the mold.

• **Cool the melted soap.** After melting the soap for pouring, stir it to cool it before pouring into the mold.

• **Start small.** Most recipes in this book make small batches (two to three bars). Making a small batch is a good way to get used to the technique.

• **Relax!** Don't worry about getting the placement perfect; the soaps are intended to be whimsical.

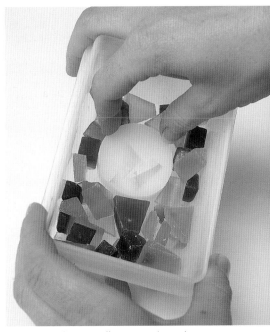

Photo 5 - Place smaller soap pieces in a larger mold to create a picture in a soap.

Unmolding Soap from Tube Molds

The soap must be completely cooled and hardened before you attempt to push it out of the mold. Hardening times vary, depending on the size of the mold and how much soap was poured in. Soap releases more easily after 24 hours. You can also place the tube mold in the refrigerator for 10 minutes. The soap should come out easily.

Here are the steps:

1. Remove the plastic wrap.
2. *Larger molds* - Use a smaller tube mold to push out solid soap from a larger tube mold. (photo 6) Always place a crumpled paper towel in the mold before pushing out the soap to prevent damaging the soap. Squeeze the mold a bit to help release the soap from the sides of the mold.

Smaller molds - Smaller molds are harder to release. Place a piece of crumpled paper towel or a coin on the soap and use a wooden dowel to push out the hardened soap. **Never use** a knife, fork, or other sharp utensil to push out the soap – you could injure yourself or damage the soap.

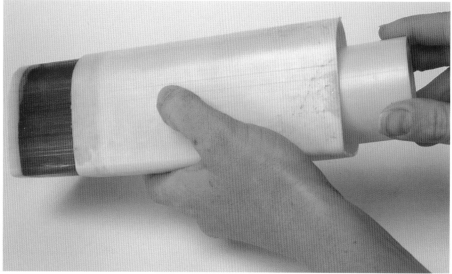

Photo 6: Remove soap from a tube mold by pushing it out with a smaller tube mold.

Slicing Soap into Bars

Use a large, non-serrated knife or a soap cutter to slice the tube of soap into bars. The soap in smaller molds can be sliced 1/2" thick. The soap made in medium and large molds should be cut 3/4" to 1" thick. Soap molded in large circle and large rectangle tube molds can be cut in half to create half circle or smaller rectangular bars.

Photo 7: Slicing soap with a knife.

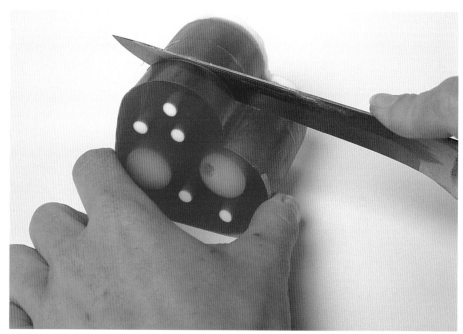

Here's how:

1. Slice off the soap plug and the top of the tube of soap. (Save these pieces; they can be re-melted and used again.)

2. Measure the soap to determine how many slices you will cut and how thick the slices will be. Mark the soap lightly with the knife to guide you.

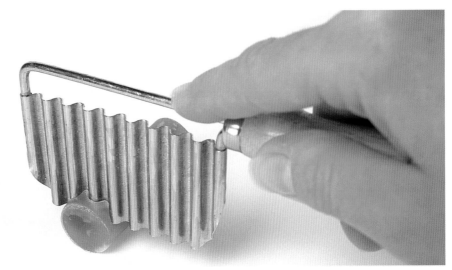

Photo 8: Slicing soap with a wavy soap cutter.

POLKA-DOT HEARTS
Red Heart with White Polka Dots

SUPPLIES

Makes three soap slices, 1" thick.

Melt & Pour Base: 3 oz. white soap base, 12 oz. clear glycerin soap base

Colorant: 6 drops red

Fragrance: 20 drops cinnamon

Molds: 1" circle tube, 3" heart tube

Other Supplies: 5 plastic straws

HERE'S HOW

1. Prepare molds with petroleum jelly and soap plug. *See "Making Picture Soaps - Techniques for Success" for detailed information on preparing mold.*

2. Melt 2 oz. white soap base. Pour in prepared 1" circle tube mold. Let set and release.

3. Cut tube in half, making two 3" white soap tubes. (photo 1)

4. Place pieces in prepared heart tube mold. (photo 2)

5. Push 5 straws in the soap plug around the white soap pieces. (photo 3)

6. Chill the mold and soap pieces in the refrigerator for 10 minutes.

7. Melt 12 oz. clear glycerin soap. Add 6 drops red colorant and 20 drops cinnamon fragrance oil. Pour in heart tube mold around straws. (photo 4) Pour just slightly over the top of the white columns. Let set.

Continued on page 38

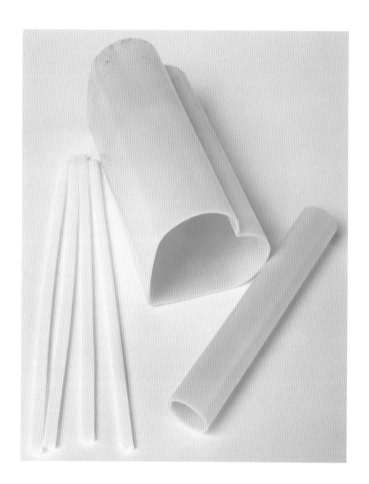

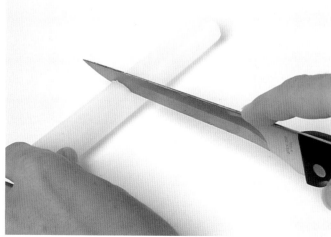

Photo 1 - Cut the pre-molded white soap tube in half.

36

Photo 2 - Place white column pieces in heart tube mold.

Photo 3 - Push the straws in the soap plug.

Photo 4 - Pour in melted red soap.

Continued from page 36

8. Remove straws. (photo 5)

9. Melt 1 oz. white soap base. Pour into holes left by straws. (photo 6) Let set.

10. Unmold. (photo 7)

11. Slice into bars. (photo 8) ❏

Photo 5 - Remove the straws.

Photo 6 - Pour melted white soap into holes left by straws.

Photo 7 - Unmold the soap.

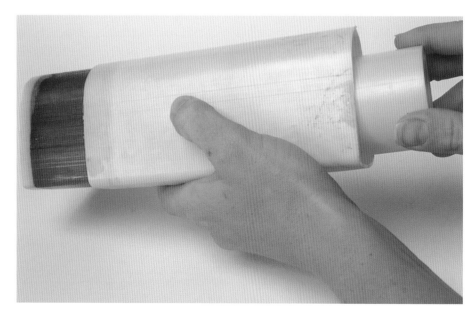

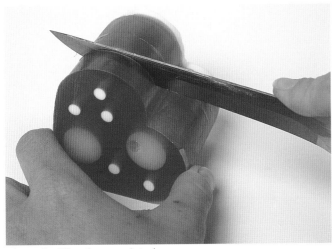

Photo 8 - Slice the soap into bars.

VARIATIONS

▨ Red Polka Dots in a White Heart

SUPPLIES

Makes three soap slices, 1" thick.

Melt & Pour Base: 3 oz. clear red glycerin soap base, 12 oz. white soap base

Fragrance: 20 drops peppermint

Molds: 1" circle tube, 3" heart tube

Other Supplies: 5 plastic straws

HERE'S HOW

See Red Heart with White Polka Dots and follow these instructions:

1. Pour 2 oz. clear red soap base in a prepared 1" circle tube mold. Let set and release. Cut tube in half, making two 3" clear red soap tubes.
2. Place the cooled red circle pieces in a prepared 3" heart tube mold. Push 5 plastic straws into the prepared soap plug. Pour in 12 oz. white glycerin soap with 20 drops peppermint fragrance oil. Remove straws.
3. Pour in 1 oz. melted clear red soap in holes. Let set. Unmold. Slice.

▨ Colored Polka Dots in a White Heart

SUPPLIES

Makes three soap slices, 1" thick.

Melt & Pour Base: 4 oz. clear glycerin soap base, 12 oz. white soap base

Colorants: red, yellow, blue

Fragrance: 20 drops coconut

Molds: 1" circle tube, 3" heart tube

Other Supplies: 5 plastic straws

HERE'S HOW

See Red Heart with White Polka Dots and follow these instructions:

1. Pour 2 oz. clear yellow soap base in a prepared small circle tube mold. Let set and release. Cut tube in half, making two 3" clear yellow soap tubes.
2. Pour 1 oz. clear red soap base into prepared small circle tube mold. Let set and release.
3. Place the cooled yellow and red circle pieces in a prepared 3" heart tube mold. Push 5 plastic straws in the prepared soap plug. Pour in 12 oz. white glycerin soap with 20 drops coconut fragrance oil. Let set. Remove straws.
4. Pour in 1 oz. melted clear blue soap in holes. Let set. Unmold. Slice. ❏

MARTINI SOAP

SUPPLIES

This makes three soap slices, 1" thick.

Melt & Pour Base: 15 oz. clear glycerin soap base, 14 oz. white soap base

Colorants: 3 drops green, 2 drops white, 2 drops red

Fragrance: 20 drops lime, 20 drops lemon

Molds: 1" circle tube, 3" heart tube, 3" x 4" rectangle tube

Other Supplies: plastic straw

HERE'S HOW

1. Prepare molds with mold release and soap plugs. *See "Making Picture Soaps - Techniques for Success" for detailed information on preparing mold.*

2. Push a straw into the prepared soap plug of a 1" circle tube mold. Pour in 2 oz. clear soap base with 3 drops green, 2 drops white, and 1 drop red colorant to make an olive hue. Let set.

3. Pull out straw and fill hole with 1/2 oz. clear soap base with 1 drop red colorant. Let set and release.

4. Unmold. Place olive column in the prepared heart tube mold at the pointed end. Chill the mold and soap piece in the refrigerator for 10 minutes.

Continued on page 42

There is no limit to the designs you can make with tube molds!

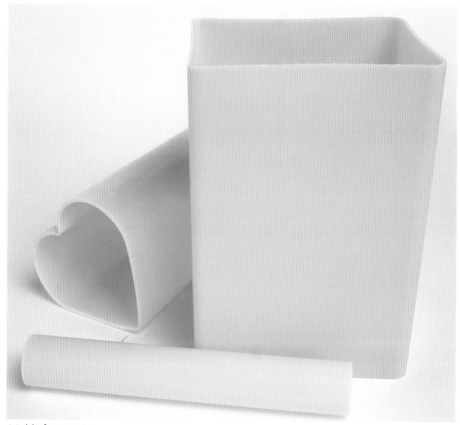

Molds for Martini soap

The "olive" tube soap, sliced to show how the finished olive will look.

continued from page 40

5. Pour in 12 oz. clear soap with 20 drops lime fragrance oil. Let set and release.

6. Cut the clear heart column in half to form the top of the martini glass. Cut the stem and the bottom of the glass from the leftover clear soap.

7. Place pieces in the 3" x 4" rectangle tube mold, arranging to form a glass. Chill mold and soap pieces.

8. Pour in white soap base with 20 drops lemon fragrance oil.

9. Let set. Unmold. Slice into bars. ❑

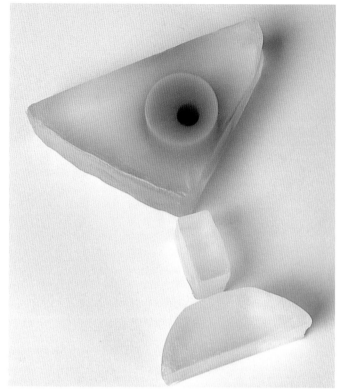

The pieces that make up the martini glass and olive for Martini soap.

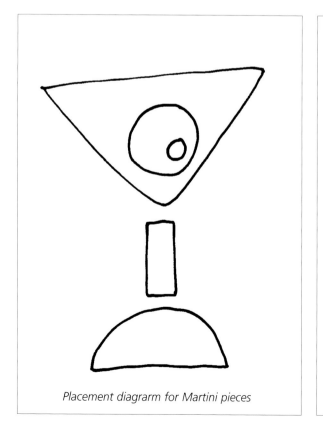

Placement diagrarm for Martini pieces

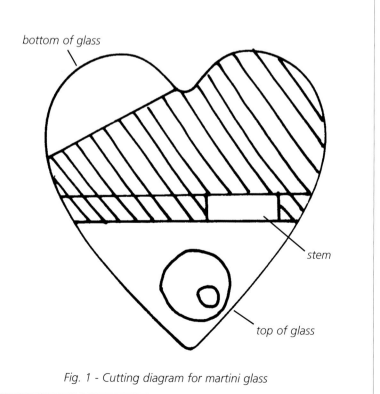

Fig. 1 - Cutting diagram for martini glass

bottom of glass

stem

top of glass

FORE!

This picture soap made in a loaf mold is sure to be a hit with golf enthusiasts. Notice how the placement of the pieces is different than working with tube molds. The pieces will be stacked and the picture will run horizontally in the mold. There are four moldings in all: the grass, the golf tee, the golf ball, and the final loaf, pictured on page 45.

SUPPLIES

Makes four 1" thick slices.

Melt & Pour Base: 12 oz. clear glycerin soap base, 12 oz. white glycerin soap base

Colorants: 4 drops green, 4 drops orange, 2 black

Fragrances: 20 drops pine, 20 drops rain

Molds: 3-1/4" x 4-3/4" x 2-1/2" loaf, 3" square, 1-1/2" star tube, 2" circle tube

Photo 1 - Pour green soap base in a square mold.

Photo 2 - Cut the green soap to make the "grass."

Photo 3 - Place the green "grass" pieces in the loaf mold.

HERE'S HOW

1. Prepare loaf mold with a petroleum jelly.

2. Melt 5 oz. clear soap base and add 4 drops green colorant. Pour melted green soap in a 3" square mold. (photo 1) Let set. Release.

3. Cut the green soap into 1/2" irregular pieces. (photo 2) This will be the grass of the finished soap.

4. Arrange green pieces in the bottom of the loaf mold to represent the grass. (photo 3)

5. To make the golf tee, melt 4 oz. white soap with 4 drops orange and 2 drops black (to make brown). Pour melted soap into the 1-1/2" star tube mold. Let set. Release. (photo 4)

6. Following the cutting diagram (Fig. 1), trim to a 4" long soap column. (photo 5, photo 6)

7. Place brown golf tee piece in the green soap pieces in the loaf mold. (photo 7)

8. To make the golf ball, cut pieces of clear soap base and place in a prepared 2" circle tube mold.

Continued on page 46

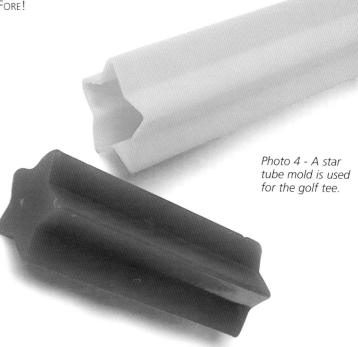

Photo 4 - A star tube mold is used for the golf tee.

Photo 7 - Place the golf tee in the mold.

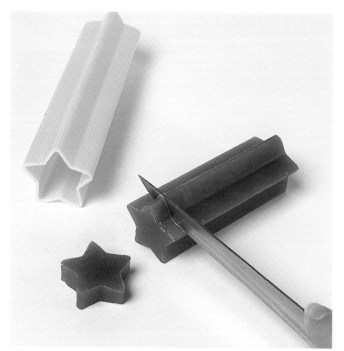

Photos 5 & 6 - Cut the golf tee column to the proper length. Trim the column into the golf tee shape. For clarity, the photo shows cutting a small piece and not the long column as you should do.

Fig. 1 - Cutting diagram for golf tee piece

Continued from page 44

9. Melt 6 oz. white soap base and add 20 drops pine fragrance oil. Pour melted soap around soap pieces in circle mold. Let set. Trim soap to make a 4" piece. (photo 8)

10. Place golf ball piece in the loaf mold over the tee and green soap pieces. (photo 9) Chill the mold and the soap pieces in the refrigerator for 10 minutes.

11. Pour 6 oz. melted clear soap with 20 drops rain fragrance oil in loaf mold around soap pieces. Do not pour to top of mold, allow golf ball to be above the level of clear soap. (photo 10)

12. Let set. Unmold. Slice into bars. ❏

Photo 8 - A round tubular mold is used for the golf ball.

Photo 9

Photo 10

These two photos show a variation on the placement of the ball and tee soap pieces. When placing the pieces vertically in mold this way, you will create one or two bars and the filler soap will enclose the ball – i.e. the ball will not protrude from the top of the bar. To create the look as shown on page 45, place the ball and tee soap tube pieces horizontally in the mold as shown in the drawing at right. Pour the filler soap about two thirds up the side of the ball, allow the top of the ball to be dimensional at top.

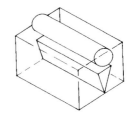

Golf Ball Soap & Bath Salts Presentation

This presentation is a perfect favor for a golf tournament and makes a great craft sale item for men. Clear tape holds the presentation in place – it is invisible in the cellophane bag and prevents the golf tee from piercing the bag.

The soap:
Make the golf ball soap according to the Fore! soap instructions, steps 7 and 8. Cut into slices 1" thick. Wrap in clear plastic wrap.

The bath salts:
Mix three tablespoons each of Epsom salts and rock salt with 20 drops rain fragrance oil and 4 drops green colorant.

The package:
Position a wooden golf tee in a clear cellophane bag and tape in place with clear tape. Pour in the bath salts. Roll a piece of clear tape to make a circle and place on top of the wrapped golf ball soap. Place in bag behind golf tee and press to adhere in place. Finish the bag with a green raffia bow and a golf ball tag. ❑

Star Flowers

Changing the color of the star flowers can vary the look of this loaf-style soap.

SUPPLIES

This makes four soap slices, 1" thick.

Melt & Pour Base: 12 oz. clear soap base, 10 oz. white

Colorants: 10 drops yellow, 4 drops green

Fragrance: 30 drops honey, 20 drops ylang-ylang

Molds: 1-1/2" star tube, 3-1/4" x 4-3/4" x 2-1/2" loaf

Other Supplies: plastic straw

HERE'S HOW

1. Prepare molds.
2. To make the flowers, place a straw in the center of a prepared 1-1/2" star tube mold. Pour in 4 oz. clear melted soap with 5 drops yellow colorant and 15 drops honey fragrance oil. Let set.
3. Pull out straw. Pour in 1 oz. melted white soap in hole. Let set. Release soap from mold.
4. Repeat steps 1 and 2 so you have two 4" long yellow star soap pieces.
5. To make the leaves, pour 4 oz. melted clear soap with 4 drops green colorant in the 1-1/2" star tube. Let set. Release.
6. Cut soap according to Fig 1. Trim to make 4" long soap columns.
7. Place yellow star and green leaf pieces in the loaf mold. Chill the mold and the soap pieces in the refrigerator for 10 minutes.
8. Pour in 8 oz. melted white soap with 20 drops ylang-ylang fragrance oil in mold around soap pieces. Let set. Unmold. Slice. ❑

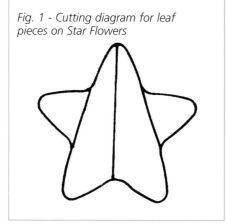

Fig. 1 - Cutting diagram for leaf pieces on Star Flowers

Flower Garden

SUPPLIES

This loaf style soap makes four soap slices, 1" thick.

Melt & Pour Base: 14 oz. white soap base, 6 oz. clear glycerin soap base

Colorants: 8 drops yellow, 5 drops red, 4 drops green

Fragrances: 10 drops rose, 10 drops violet, 15 drops ginger

Molds: 1-1/2" blossom tube, 1" circle tube, 1-1/2" heart tube, 3-1/4" x 4-3/4" x 2-1/2" loaf

Other Supplies: plastic straw

HERE'S HOW

1. Prepare molds.
2. To make the yellow flower, place a straw in the center of a 1-1/2" blossom mold. Pour in 4 oz. melted white soap with 5 drops yellow colorant and 10 drops rose fragrance oil. Let set.
3. Pull out straw. Pour in 1 oz. melted white soap with 2 drops red colorant in hole. Let set. Unmold. Trim to make a 4" long soap piece.
4. To make the pink flower, pour 2-1/2 oz. melted white soap with 3 drops yellow colorant into a 1" circle tube. Let set. Unmold.
5. Place yellow soap piece in 1-1/2" blossom mold. Chill 10 minutes.
6. Pour 2-1/2 oz. melted white soap with 3 drops red colorant and 10 drops violet fragrance oil in the blossom mold around the yellow piece. Let set. Unmold. Trim to make a 4" long soap piece.
7. To make the green leaves, pour 4 oz. melted white soap with 4 drops green colorant in a 1-1/2" heart mold. Let set.
8. Unmold. Cut in half lengthwise to make two 4" long green leaf pieces.
9. Lay blossom pieces and green leaf pieces in the loaf mold. Chill the mold and the soap pieces in the refrigerator for 10 minutes.
10. Pour in 6 oz. melted clear soap with 15 drops ginger fragrance oil into mold around soap pieces. Let set. Unmold and slice. ❑

Pictured clockwise from top left: Star Flowers, Flower Garden, Rose Impression, Pastel Stars.

ROSE IMPRESSION

Pictured on page 49

The rose and leaves are cut from circle molds for a fanciful floral design.

SUPPLIES

Makes three slices, 1" thick.

Melt & Pour Base: 12 oz. white soap base, 4 oz. clear

Colorants: 4 drops red, 4 drops green

Fragrances: 20 drops rose, 10 drops musk

Molds: 2" circle tube, 3" oval tube

HERE'S HOW

1. Prepare the molds.

2. To make the rose, pour 6 oz. white soap base with 4 drops red colorant in a 2" circle tube mold. Let set. Release.

3. Cut into six pieces, using Fig. 1 as a guide.

4. To make the leaves, pour 6 oz. white soap base with 4 drops green colorant in a 2" circle tube mold. Let set. Release.

5. Cut into leaf pieces, using Fig. 2 as a guide.

6. Place the rose and leaf soap column pieces into a 3" oval tube mold. Chill mold and soap pieces in refrigerator for 10 minutes.

7. Pour in 4 oz. clear soap base with 20 drops rose fragrance oil and 10 drops musk fragrance oil around chilled pieces. Let set. Unmold, trim, and slice. ❑

PASTEL STARS

Pictured on page 49

A small star is centered within a larger star. The recipe given is for just two soap slices, but since these are tube molds, you can increase the amounts, filling the tube higher to make more slices.

SUPPLIES

This recipe makes two soap slices, 3/4" thick.

Melt & Pour Base: 5 oz. white soap base

Colorants: 3 drops blue, 3 drops red

Fragrance: 20 drops mulberry

Molds: 1-1/2" star tube, 3" star tube

HERE'S HOW

1. Prepare molds.

2. Pour 2 oz. white soap base with 3 drops blue into a 1-1/2" star tube mold. Let set. Release.

3. Place the blue heart soap column in a prepared 3" star tube mold. Chill in the refrigerator for 10 minutes.

4. Pour in 3 oz. white soap base with 20 drops mulberry fragrance oil and 3 drops red colorant. Let set. Unmold, trim, and slice. ❑

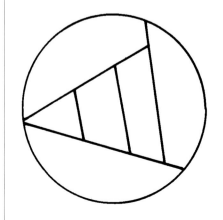

Fig. 1 - Cutting diagram for rose pieces for Rose Impression

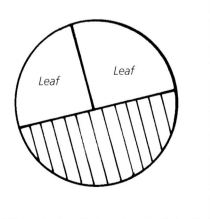

Fig. 2 - Cutting diagram for leaf pieces for Rose Impression

Leaf

Leaf

CUCUMBER MINT

Pictured on page 53

SUPPLIES

Makes four slices, 1" thick.

Melt & Pour Base: 6 oz. white coconut oil soap base, 6 oz. clear glycerin soap base

Colorants: 6 drops green

Fragrance: 30 drops cucumber, 20 drops peppermint

Molds: 2 " circle tube, 2-3/4" circle tube

Other Supplies: 3 plastic straws

HERE'S HOW

1. Prepare the molds.

2. Press 3 plastic straws between your fingers to form them into flattened ovals. Press the straws into the base of the 2" circle tube mold.

3. Melt 6 oz. white soap base. Add 30 drops cucumber fragrance and pour into mold around the straws. Let set and release.

4. Place the white soap column in a 2-3/4" circle tube mold. Chill mold and soap pieces in the refrigerator for 10 minutes.

5. Melt 6 oz. clear glycerin soap base. Add 20 drops peppermint fragrance oil and 6 drops green colorant. Remove the straws.

6. Pour melted clear green soap around the edge and in the holes created by the straws. Let set. Unmold. Trim and slice. ❑

BRILLIANT NIGHT

Pictured on page 53

Three smaller stars float within clear blue-sky background. This design is created with tube molds.

SUPPLIES

Makes three soap slices, 1" thick.

Melt & Pour Base: 9 oz. white coconut oil soap base, 8 oz. clear glycerin soap base

Colorants: 5 drops yellow, 9 drops blue, 4 drops green

Fragrances: 15 drops honey, 20 drops musk

Molds: 1-1/2" star tube, 3-1/2" circle tube

HERE'S HOW

1. Prepare molds.

2. To make the stars, pour 3 oz. white melted soap with 5 drops yellow colorant and 5 drops honey fragrance oil in a prepared 1-1/2" star tube mold Let set. Unmold.

3. Repeat twice so you have three 3" long star-shaped soap pieces. Add 4 drops blue to one molding and 4 drops green to the other.

4. Place the three star shapes in a 3-1/2" circle tube mold. Chill the mold and the soap pieces in the refrigerator for 10 minutes.

5. Melt 8 oz. clear soap and add 5 drops blue colorant and 20 drops musk fragrance oil. Pour in the mold around the star-shaped soap pieces. Let set. Unmold. Trim and slice. ❑

FISH BOWL

This soap features a green fish swimming in a translucent blue sea with clear bubbles.

SUPPLIES

It makes three soap slices, 3/4" thick.

Melt & Pour Base: 11 oz. clear, 1/2 oz. whitened glycerin soap base

Colorants: 3 drops green, 3 drops white, 4 drops blue

Fragrance: 20 drops ocean

Molds: 1-1/2" heart tube, 1-1/2" circle tube, 2-2/4" circle tube

Other Supplies: 6 plastic straws

HERE'S HOW

1. Prepare the molds.

2. To make the green fish, push a straw into the soap plug of a 1-1/2" heart tube mold. Pour in 4 oz. clear soap base with 3 drops green. Let set.

3. Pull out straw and fill hole with 1/2 oz. white soap base with 1 drop blue colorant. Let set and release.

4. Cut soap according to Fig. 1. Trim to make 4" long soap column.

5. To make the clear bubbles, pour 2 oz. clear soap in a 1-1/2" circle tube mold. Let set. Release.

6. Cut the soap tube in half to create two clear soap columns.

7. Place fish pieces and bubble pieces in a prepared 2-3/4" circle tube mold, using Fig. 2 as a guide. Push 4 to 5 plastic straws in the soap plug. Place mold and soap pieces into refrigerator for 10 minutes to chill.

8. Melt 5 oz. of clear soap and add 3 drops white colorant and 3 drops blue colorant for a translucent blue hue. Add 20 drops ocean fragrance oil and pour in circle tube mold around soap pieces. Let set. Remove straws.

9. Melt 1 oz. of clear soap and pour into holes made by straws. Let set. Unmold.

10. Trim and slice. ❑

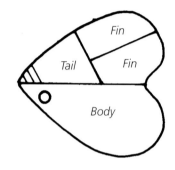

Fig. 1 - Cutting diagram for fish pieces for Fish Bowl soap

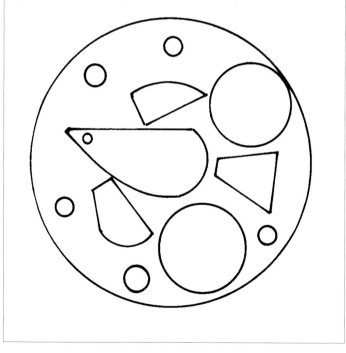

Fig. 2 - Placement diagram for Fish Bowl soap

Pictured on page 53, clockwise from left: Cucumber Mint, Brilliant Night, Fish Bowl.

VARIATIONS

Goldfish

SUPPLIES

Makes three soap slices, 3/4" thick.

Melt & Pour Base: 11 oz. clear, 1/2 oz. whitened glycerin soap base

Colorants: 3 drops white, 4 drops blue, 1 drop red, 2 drops yellow, gold glitter powder

Fragrance: 20 drops ocean

Molds: 1-1/2" heart tube, 1-1/2" circle tube, 2-2/4" circle tube

Other Supplies: 6 plastic straws

Follow the instructions for Fish Bowl, but color the fish with red and yellow colorants (to make orange) and add gold glitter powder for extra sparkle.

53

SWEET BUNNY

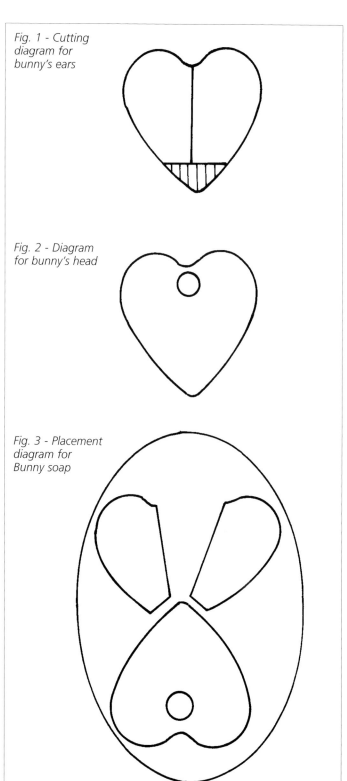

Fig. 1 - Cutting diagram for bunny's ears

Fig. 2 - Diagram for bunny's head

Fig. 3 - Placement diagram for Bunny soap

SUPPLIES

Makes four bars, 3/4" thick.

Melt & Pour Base: 8 oz. white glycerin soap base, 6 oz. clear glycerin soap base

Fragrance: 20 drops honey almond

Colorant: 4 drops red

Molds: 1-1/2" heart tube, 3" oval tube

Other Supplies: plastic straw, soap paint for eyes

HERE'S HOW

1. To make bunny's ears, pour 4 oz. white soap base in a prepared 1-1/2" heart mold. Let set and release.
2. Slice heart lengthwise to make two bars. See Fig. 1.
3. To make the bunny's face, push a plastic straw in the base of a 1-1/2" tube mold to create a hole for the nose. See. Fig. 2. Melt 4 oz. white soap base and pour around the straw. Let set. Release.
4. Arrange the cooled white pieces in a prepared 3" oval tube mold to form the head of a bunny. See Fig. 3.
5. Pour in 6 oz. clear soap base with 4 drops red colorant and 20 drops honey almond fragrance oil around soap pieces and in the nose hole. Let set and release.
6. Trim ends and slice soap into 3/4" thick bars.
7. Add two dots with soap paint to create the eyes.

Pictured on page 55, left to right: Sweet Bunny, Pastel Hearts, Butterfly. Instructions follow on pages 56 & 57.

PASTEL HEARTS

Pictured on page 55

SUPPLIES

Makes two bars, 3/4" thick.

Melt & Pour Base: 5 oz. clear glycerin soap base

Fragrance: 15 drops bubble gum

Colorants: 6 drops white, 3 drops red, 2 drops blue

Molds: 1-1/2" heart tube, 3" heart tube

HERE'S HOW

1. Pour 2 oz. clear soap base with 3 drops white and 3 drops red colorant in a prepared 1-1/2" heart tube mold. Let set and release. Cool.

2. Place the cooled pink heart soap column in a prepared 3" heart tube mold. Pour in 3 oz. clear soap base with 20 drops baby powder fragrance oil, 3 drops white colorant, and 2 drops blue colorant. Let set and release.

3. Trim soap and slice into two 3/4" thick bars. ❏

FLOWER POWER

Pictured on page 59

SUPPLIES

This recipe, courtesy Environmental Technologies, makes two slices, 1" thick.

Melt & Pour Base: 5 oz. clear glycerin soap base

Fragrance: 15 drops honeysuckle

Colorants: 7 drops yellow, 2 drops white, 3 drops red

Molds: 1-1/2" star tube, 3" oval tube

HERE'S HOW

1. Pour 1 oz. clear soap base with 3 drops yellow and 2 drops white colorant in a prepared 1.75" round tube mold. Let set and release. Cool.

2. Place cooled yellow soap column in a prepared 3" blossom tube mold. Pour in 4 oz. clear soap base with 15 drops honeysuckle fragrance oil, 3 drops red colorant, and 4 drops yellow colorant. Let set and release.

3. Trim ends and slice into two 1" thick bars. ❏

BUTTERFLY

Pictured on page 55

SUPPLIES

This recipe, courtesy Environmental Technologies, makes two bars, 3/4" thick.

Melt & Pour Base: 8 oz. clear glycerin soap base

Fragrance: 10 drops eucalyptus therapy

Colorants: 4 drops white, 4 drops blue

Molds: 1-1/2" heart tube, butterfly tube

HERE'S HOW

1. Pour 3 oz. clear soap base and 4 drops blue colorant in a prepared 1-1/2" heart mold. Let set and release.

2. Slice heart column into two bars. Then cut each piece in half lengthwise. Cut a notch from two pieces of the half hearts. See Fig. 1.

3. Arrange the pieces in the butterfly mold to form wings. See Fig. 2.

4. Pour in 6 oz. clear soap base with 4 drops white colorant and 10 drops eucalyptus therapy fragrance oil. Let set and release.

5. Trim ends and slice soap into two 3/4" thick bars. ❏

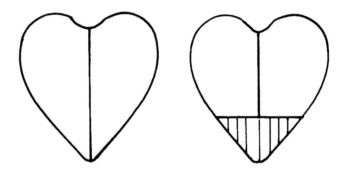

Fig. 1 - Cutting diagram for Butterfly soap

Fig. 2 - Placement diagram for Butterfly soap

DAISY FRESH

SUPPLIES

This recipe, courtesy Environmental Technologies, makes two bars, 1" thick.

Melt & Pour Base: 8 oz. clear glycerin soap base

Fragrance: flower scent

Colorants: 2 drops yellow, 5 drops white, 3 drops blue

Molds: 1-3/4" round tube, 1-1/2" heart tube, 3" blossom tube

HERE'S HOW

1. Pour 1 oz. clear soap base with 2 drops yellow colorant and 1 drop white colorant in a prepared 1-3/4" round tube mold. Let set. Release.

2. Pour 4 oz. clear soap base with 4 drops white colorant in a prepared 1-1/2" heart tube mold. Let set. Release.

3. Cut white heart soap column into three 2" slices. Cut in half length-wise and trim off points to form 6 petals. Cool.

4. Arrange the cooled yellow soap column in the center surrounded by the 6 white petals in a prepared 3" blossom mold.

5. Pour in 3 oz. clear soap base with 3 drops blue colorant. Let set. Release. Trim soap and slice into two 1" thick bars. ❑

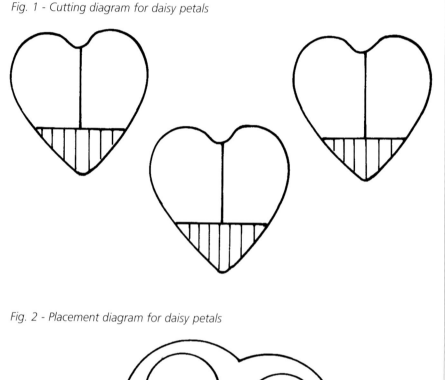

Fig. 1 - Cutting diagram for daisy petals

Fig. 2 - Placement diagram for daisy petals

Pictured on next page, clockwise from top left: Oval Floral, Flower Power, Daisy Fresh, Mini Flower Power with Leaves

MINI FLOWER POWER WITH LEAVES

Pictured on page 59

These small soaps can be arranged on a soap dish for a pretty display.

SUPPLIES

The recipe makes two bars, 3/4" thick.

Melt & Pour Base: 5 oz. clear glycerin soap base

Fragrance: 10 drops jasmine

Colorants: 3 drops yellow, 4 drops white, 3 drops green

Molds: 1-1/2" blossom tube, 1-1/2" heart tube

Other Supplies: Red soap paint

SUPPLIES

1. Pour 3 oz. clear soap base with 10 drops jasmine fragrance oil, 3 drops yellow colorant, and 2 drops white colorant in a prepared 1-1/2" blossom tube mold. Let set and release.

2. Pour 2 oz. clear soap base, 3 drops green colorant, and 2 drops white colorant in a prepared 1-1/2" heart mold. Let set and release.

3. Cut the heart in half to create the leaves.

4. Cut soap flowers and leaves into 3/4" thick slices.

5. Paint a red dot at the center of each flower. ❑

OVAL FLORAL

Pictured on page 59

SUPPLIES

Makes two bars, 1" thick.

Melt & Pour Base: 10-1/2 oz. clear glycerin soap base

Colorants: 3 drops white, 1 drop red, 3 drops blue

Fragrance: 20 drops lilac

Molds: 1-1/2" blossom tube, 1-1/2" heart tube, 3" oval tube

Other Supplies: 1 plastic straw

HERE'S HOW

1. Prepare molds.

2. To make the flower, push a straw in the base of a 1-1/2" blossom tube mold. Pour in 2 oz. clear soap base with 3 drops white colorant. Let set.

3. Pull out straw. To make the flower center, pour in 1/2 oz. of melted soap base with 1 drop red colorant. Let set. Release.

4. To make the leaves, pour 3 oz. clear soap base with 3 drops green colorant and 2 drops white colorant in a 1-1/2" heart tube mold. Let set and release.

5. Cut the green heart column in half to create the two leaves.

6. Arrange the white blossom soap column and the two green leaf soap columns in a 3" oval mold. Chill in the refrigerator for 10 minutes.

7. Pour in 5 oz. clear soap base with 20 drops lilac fragrance oil and 3 drops blue colorant. Let set and release.

8. Trim soap and slice into two 1" thick bars. ❑

KIWI SLICE

Pictured on page 63

SUPPLIES

This makes two bars, 1" thick.

Melt & Pour Base: 8 oz. clear glycerin soap base

Fragrance: 20 drops kiwi

Colorants: 3 drops white, 4 drops green

Additive: 1/2 teaspoon poppy seeds

Molds: 1-1/2" star tube, 2-1/2" tube

HERE'S HOW

1. Pour 2 oz. clear glycerin soap base and 3 drops white colorant in prepared 1-1/2" star mold. Let set and release.

2. Place cooled white star in prepared 2-1/2" tube mold and pour in 6 oz. clear glycerin soap base with 4 drops green colorant, 20 drops kiwi fragrance oil, and 1/2 teaspoon poppy seeds. Let set and release.

3. Trim ends and slice soap into two bars 1" thick. ❑

WATERMELON SLICE

Pictured on page 63

SUPPLIES

This recipe, courtesy Environmental Technologies, makes two bars, 1" thick – four if the circles are cut in half.

Melt & Pour Base: 10 oz. clear glycerin soap base

Fragrance: 20 drops watermelon

Colorants: 5 drops red, 3 drops black, 3 drops white, 2 drops green

Molds: 2" tube, 2-1/2" tube

Other Supplies: 5 plastic straws

HERE'S HOW

1. Push 5 straws in the prepared base of 2" round tube mold. Melt 5 oz. clear glycerin soap base. Add 20 drops watermelon fragrance oil and 5 drops red colorant. Pour in 2" tube mold around straws. Let set.

2. Pull out the plastic straws. Pour 1 oz. clear glycerin soap base with 3 drops black colorant into holes. Let set and release.

3. Place red soap column in prepared 2-1/2" tube mold. Pour in 4 oz. clear soap with 3 drops white colorant. Let set and release.

4. Trim 1/4" of white soap away all around column. Place back in prepared 2-1/2" tube mold.

5. Pour in 2 oz. clear soap base with 2 drops green colorant. Let set and release.

6. Trim ends and slice soap into two 1" bars. Cut bars in half to make 4 watermelon slices. ❑

STRAWBERRY HEART

SUPPLIES

This recipe, courtesy Environmental Technologies, makes two bars, 1" thick.

Melt & Pour Base: 10 oz. clear glycerin soap base

Fragrance: 20 drops strawberry shortcake

Colorants: 4 drops red, 3 drops green, 5 drops white

Molds: 1-1/2" star tube, 3" heart tube

Other Supplies: 8 plastic straws

HERE'S HOW

1. Pour 2 oz. clear soap base with 3 drops green and 2 drops white colorant in prepared 1-1/2" star mold. Let set and release.

2. Trim one point off the green star soap column. Place at top of prepared 3" heart tube mold. Push 8 plastic straws in the prepared base. Pour in 6 oz. clear soap base with 20 drops strawberry shortcake fragrance oil and 4 drops red colorant around straws.

3. Remove straws. Pour 2 oz. clear soap base with 3 drops white colorant into holes. Let set and release.

4. Trim ends and slice soap in two 1" thick bars. ❑

STAR FRUIT

SUPPLIES

Makes two bars, 1" thick.

Melt & Pour Base: 8 oz. clear glycerin soap base

Fragrance: 20 drops mango

Colorants: 6 drops yellow, 3 drops white

Molds: 1-1/2" star tube, 3" star tube

HERE'S HOW

1. Pour 2 oz. clear soap base with 3 drops white colorant in prepared 1-1/2" star mold. Let set and release. Cool.

2. Place cooled white star soap column in prepared 3" star tube mold. Pour in 6 oz. clear soap base with 6 drops yellow colorant and 20 drops mango fragrance oil. Let set and release.

3. Trim ends and slice soap into two 1" thick bars. ❑

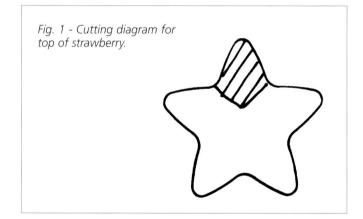

Fig. 1 - Cutting diagram for top of strawberry.

Pictured clockwise from top left: Kiwi Slice, Strawberry Heart, Star Fruit, Watermelon Slice.

BEE

SUPPLIES

Makes two bars, 3/4" thick.

Melt & Pour Base: 8 oz. clear glycerin soap base

Fragrance: 15 drops honey

Colorants: 4 drops white, 4 drops yellow, 4 drops black

Additive: Tiny pinch of gold glitter

Molds: 2" round tube, 3" heart tube

HERE'S HOW

1. Pour 3 oz. clear soap base with 4 drops white, 4 drops yellow, and 1 drop black colorant (to make an amber hue) in a prepared 2" round tube mold. Let set and release.

2. Trim a 1/4" piece off the end of the amber soap column for the bee's head. Cut circle in half and make notches in each side to form the zigzag stripes. See Fig. 1. Cool.

3. Place the cooled pieces in the prepared 2" round tube mold. Pour in 2 oz. clear soap base with 3 drops black colorant. Let set and release.

4. Place the bee body in a prepared 3" heart mold with the black face tight into the point of the heart.

5. Pour in 3 oz. clear soap base with 15 drops honey and a tiny pinch of gold glitter. Let set and release.

6. Trim ends and slice soap into two 3/4" thick bars. ❏

LADYBUG

SUPPLIES

Makes three bars, 3/4" thick.

Melt & Pour Base: 5 oz. clear glycerin soap base

Fragrance: 10 drops blackberry

Colorants: 6 drops red, 2 drops white, 3 drops black

Molds: 2" round tube

Other Supplies: 4 plastic straws

HERE'S HOW

1. Push 4 straws in a prepared 2" round tube mold. Pour in 4 oz. clear soap base with 6 drops red colorant, 2 drops white colorant, and 15 drops blackberry fragrance oil. Let set and release.

2. Pull out the straws. Cut a 1/4" slice from the red column. (This is the ladybug's head.) Cut a narrow notch at the back. See Fig. 1.

3. Arrange the red column soap piece back in the round mold. Pour in 1 oz. clear soap base with 3 drops black colorant into spaces and holes from straws. Let set and release.

4. Trim ends and slice soap into three 3/4" thick bars. ❏

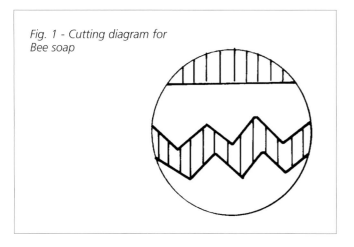

Fig. 1 - Cutting diagram for Bee soap

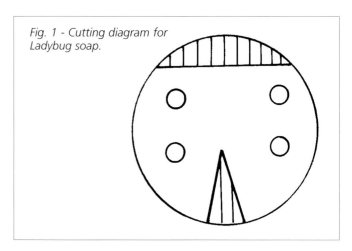

Fig. 1 - Cutting diagram for Ladybug soap.

Pictured clockwise from top left: Glitter Star, Patriotic Bar, Ladybug, Bee.

Glitter Star

Pictured on page 65

SUPPLIES

This recipe, courtesy Environmental Technologies, makes four bars, 1" thick.

Melt & Pour Base: 10 oz. clear glycerin soap base

Fragrance: 20 drops bubble gum

Additive: 1/2 teaspoon multi-colored glitter slivers

Mold: 3" plastic star tube

HERE'S HOW

1. Prepare mold.

2. Melt soap base. Add fragrance and glitter. Stir the soap until it cools and thickens slightly to distribute the glitter throughout the soap.

3. Pour in mold. Let set. Unmold. Slice. ❏

Patriotic Bar

Pictured on page 65

SUPPLIES

Makes two bars, 1" thick.

Melt & Pour Base: 13 oz. clear glycerin soap base

Fragrances: 10 drops apple spice, 10 drops vanilla

Colorants: 6 drops white, 4 drops blue, 4 drops red

Molds: 1-1/2" star tube, 3" oval tube

HERE'S HOW

1. Pour 2 oz. clear soap base with 3 drops white colorant in a prepared 1-1/2" star tube mold. Let set and release. Cool.

2. Place cooled star soap column at one end of a prepared 3" oval tube mold. Pour in 5 oz. clear soap base with 4 drops blue colorant and 10 drops apple spice fragrance oil. Let set and release.

3. Cut the oval soap column in half at an angle and place back in the prepared 3" oval tube mold.

4. Pour in 3 oz. clear soap base with 10 drops vanilla fragrance oil and 4 drops red colorant. Let set and release.

5. Slice the red part of the oval soap column to create stripes.

6. Place the pieces back into the prepared 3" oval tube mold and pour in 3 oz. clear soap base with 3 drops white colorant. Let set and release.

7. Trim soap and slice into two 1" thick bars. ❏

RAIN CLOUD

Pictured on page 69

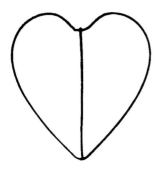

Fig. 1 - Cutting diagram for cloud

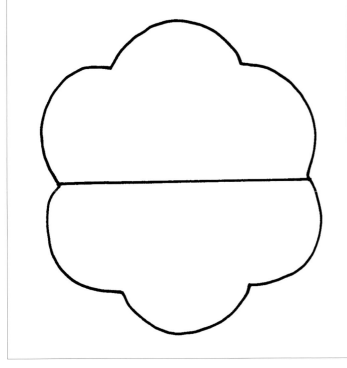

Fig. 2 - Cutting diagram for raindrops

SUPPLIES

Makes four bars, 1" thick.

Melt & Pour Base: 10 oz. clear glycerin soap base, 8 oz. white glycerin soap base

Colorant: 4 drops blue

Fragrance: 30 drops rainforest

Molds: 1-1/2" heart tube, 3" blossom tube

HERE'S HOW

1. To make the raindrops, pour 4 oz. clear soap base with 2 drops blue colorant in a prepared 1-1/2" heart tube mold. Let set and release.

2. To make the cloud, pour 8 oz. white soap base and 30 drops rainforest fragrance oil in a prepared 3" blossom tube mold. Let set and release.

3. Cut the white blossom soap column in half. Place half in a prepared blossom mold. See Fig. 1.

4. Cut the blue heart in half to create two raindrops. See Fig. 2.

5. Arrange raindrops in blossom mold with white cloud piece. Place in refrigerator to chill for 10 minutes.

6. Pour in 6 oz. clear soap base with 2 drops blue colorant. Let set and release. Trim soap and slice into four 1" thick bars. ❏

RAINBOW

SUPPLIES

This recipe, courtesy Environmental Technologies, makes four bars.

Melt & Pour Base: 10 oz. clear glycerin soap base

Colorants: 3 drops yellow, 3 drops red, 3 drops blue

Fragrance: 30 drops rain

Molds: 2" round tube, 2-1/2" round tube, 3" round tube

HERE'S HOW

1. Pour 3 oz. clear soap base with 10 drops rain fragrance oil and 3 drops yellow colorant in a prepared 2" round tube mold. Let set and release. Cool.

2. Place cooled yellow soap column in a prepared 2-1/2" round tube mold and pour in 3 oz. clear soap base with 3 drops red colorant and 10 drops rain fragrance oil. Let set and release. Cool.

3. Place cooled yellow and red soap column in a prepared 3" round tube mold and pour in 4 oz. clear soap base with 10 drops rain fragrance oil and 3 drops blue colorant. Let set and release.

4. Trim soap and slice into two 3/4" slices. Cut each slice in half to create four rainbow bars.

STARRY NIGHT

SUPPLIES

Makes two bars, 3/4" thick.

Melt & Pour Base: 7 oz. clear glycerin soap base

Colorants: 4 drops yellow, 4 drops blue

Fragrances: 15 drops frankincense, 5 drops jasmine

Additive: Pinch of iridescent glitter

Molds: 1-1/2" star tube, 3" oval tube

HERE'S HOW

1. Pour 3 oz. clear soap base with 4 drops yellow colorant in a prepared 1-1/2" star tube mold. Let set and release.

2. Cut the yellow star soap column in three pieces. Place in a prepared 3" oval mold. Pour in 4 oz. clear soap base with 4 drops blue colorant, a pinch of iridescent glitter, 15 drops frankincense fragrance oil, and 5 drops jasmine fragrance oil. Let set and release.

3. Trim soap and slice into two 3/4" bars. ❑

Pictured clockwise from top left: Rainbow, Starry Night, Sunshine, Rain Cloud.

SUNSHINE

Pictured on page 69

SUPPLIES

Makes two bars, 3/4" thick.

Melt & Pour Base: 5 oz. clear glycerin soap base

Colorants: 2 drops yellow, 4 drops blue, 3 drops white

Fragrances: 5 drops lavender, 10 drops lemon

Additives: Pinch of gold glitter, red and yellow soap cubes

Molds: 1.75" round tube, 2-1/2" round tube

HERE'S HOW

1. Pour 1 oz. clear soap base with 2 drops yellow colorant and a pinch of gold glitter in a prepared 1.75" round tube mold. Let set and release. Cool.

2. Place cooled yellow soap column in a prepared 2-1/2" round tube mold. Add cooled red and yellow soap cubes around yellow column.

3. Pour in 4 oz. clear soap base with 4 drops blue colorant, 3 drops white colorant, and the fragrance oils. Let set and release.

4. Trim soap and slice into two 3/4" thick bars. ❏

ORANGE SLICE

SUPPLIES

Makes four circle slices or eight half-circle slices, 3/4" thick.

Melt & Pour Base: 12 oz. clear soap base, 4 oz. white soap base

Colorants: 8 drops orange

Fragrance: 30 drops sweet orange

Molds: 2-3/4" circle tube, 3-1/2" circle tube

HERE'S HOW

1. Prepare molds.

2. Melt 12 oz. of clear soap base with 30 drops sweet orange fragrance oil and 8 drops orange colorant. Pour in 2-3/4" circle tube mold. Let set and release.

3. Cut orange soap column in six sections. See Fig of "Grapefruit Slice" on page 73. 1. Place in 3-1/2" circle tube mold. Chill mold and soap pieces in refrigerator for 10 minutes.

4. Melt 4 oz. of white soap base. Pour in and around sections. Let set, unmold, trim, and slice. ❏

See Fig. 1 of Grapefruit on page 73.

LIME SLICE

Pictured on page 71

SUPPLIES

Makes four circle slices or eight half-circle slices, 3/4" thick.

Melt & Pour Base: 12 oz. clear soap base, 4 oz. white soap base

Colorant: 6 drops green

Fragrance: 30 drops sweet lime

Molds: 2-3/4" circle tube, 3-1/2" circle tube

HERE'S HOW

1. Prepare molds.

2. Melt 12 oz. of clear soap base with 30 drops sweet lime fragrance oil and 6 drops green colorant. Pour in 2-3/4" circle tube mold. Let set and release.

3. Cut green soap column in six sections. See Fig. 1. Place in 3-1/2" circle tube mold. Chill mold and soap pieces in refrigerator for 10 minutes.

4. Melt 4 oz. of white soap base. Pour in and around sections. Let set, unmold, trim, and slice. ❑

LEMON SLICE

Pictured on page 71

SUPPLIES

Makes four circle slices or eight half-circle slices, 3/4" thick.

Melt & Pour Base: 12 oz. clear soap base, 4 oz. white soap base

Colorant: 10 drops green

Fragrance: 30 drops lemon

Molds: 2-3/4" circle tube, 3-1/2" circle tube

HERE'S HOW

1. Prepare molds.

2. Melt 12 oz. of clear soap base with 30 drops lemon fragrance oil and 10 drops yellow colorant. Pour in 2-3/4" circle tube mold. Let set and release.

3. Cut yellow soap column in six sections. See Fig. 1. Place in 3-1/2" circle tube mold. Chill mold and soap pieces in refrigerator for 10 minutes.

4. Melt 4 oz. of white soap base. Pour in and around sections. Let set, unmold, trim, and slice. ❑

PINK GRAPEFRUIT SLICE

Pictured on page 71

SUPPLIES

Makes four circle slices or eight half-circle slices, 3/4" thick.

Melt & Pour Base: 12 oz. clear soap base, 4 oz. white soap base

Colorants: 6 drops red, 3 drops white

Fragrance: 30 drops pink grapefruit

Molds: 2-3/4" circle tube, 3-1/2" circle tube

HERE'S HOW

1. Prepare molds.

2. Melt 12 oz. of clear soap base with 30 drops pink grapefruit fragrance oil, 6 drops red colorant, and 3 drops white colorant. Pour in 2-3/4" circle tube mold. Let set and release.

3. Cut pink soap column in six sections. See Fig. 1. Place in 3-1/2" circle tube mold. Chill mold and soap pieces in refrigerator for 10 minutes.

4. Melt 4 oz. of white soap base. Pour in and around sections. Let set, unmold, trim, and slice. ❑

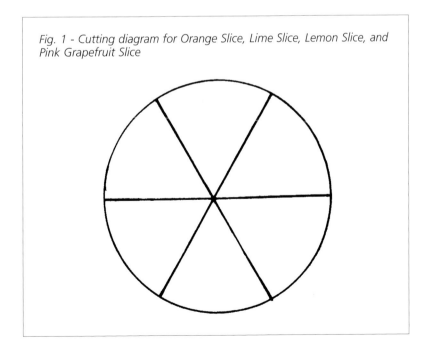

Fig. 1 - Cutting diagram for Orange Slice, Lime Slice, Lemon Slice, and Pink Grapefruit Slice

Pictured clockwise left to right: Rose Bud, Hearts, Plumaria.

Embedded Soaps

These soaps use small molded soaps embedded in a clear soap bar. The small soaps (the "embeds") are molded in small motif tray soap molds or candy molds. *(See the Supplies section for special instructions on working with candy molds.)* For best results, use a soap base with a high melting point, such as coconut oil soap base, for the small pieces and chill them in the refrigerator for 10 minutes before pouring on the clear melted soap. The Plumaria Flowers recipe is used to illustrate the embedded soap technique.

PLUMARIA

Pictured on page 74

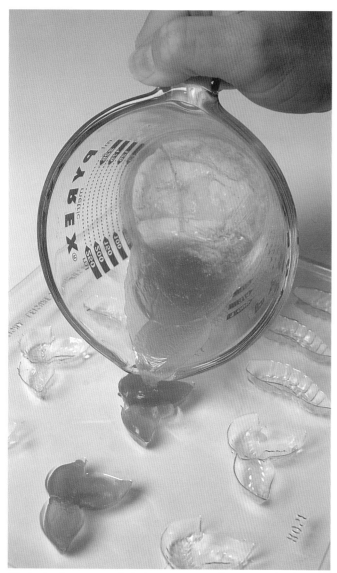

SUPPLIES

The recipe makes one bar.

Melt & Pour Base: 2 oz. clear soap base, 2 oz. white coconut oil soap base

Colorants: green

Fragrance: 10 drops plumaria

Molds: 2-1/2" domed circle, blossom and leaf candy molds

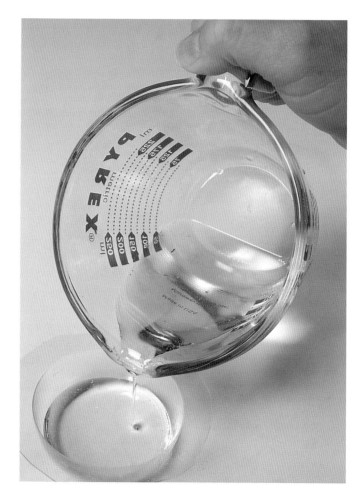

Photo 1 - Pour green-tinted coconut soap base to make the leaves.

Photo 2 - Pour a small amount of clear melted soap in the mold.

HERE'S HOW

1. Make 3 white blossoms and 1 green leaf soap with coconut oil soap, using the small motif molds. Use green colorant for the leaves. (photo 1) Let set and release. Chill the pieces in the refrigerator at least 10 minutes.

2. Melt the clear soap base and add the fragrance. Pour a small amount in the mold to fill it halfway. (photo 2) Wait until a skin has formed on the top – about a minute – and carefully remove the skin with the point of a knife. (This removes bubbles and/or foam from the top of the soap.)

3. While the clear soap is still liquid, add the chilled small soap motifs face down to the mold. (photo 3) Let the first pouring of the clear soap set a bit; then pour in melted clear soap to fill the mold.

4. Let set. Unmold. ❏

Photo 3 - Arrange the soap embeds in the mold.

ROSE BUD

Pictured on page 74

SUPPLIES

Makes 1 soap bar.

Melt & Pour Base: 4 oz. clear soap base, 4 oz. white coconut oil soap base

Colorants: red, green

Fragrance: 15 drops rose

Molds: 3-3/4" x 2-1/2" domed oval (bar), rosebud soap mold and leaf candy mold (embeds)

Use the step-by-step instructions for the Plumaria Flowers soap as a guide. Make 6 red rosebuds and 3 green leaf motifs with coconut oil soap base. ❏

HEARTS

Pictured on page 74

SUPPLIES

Makes 1 soap bar.

Melt & Pour Base: 2 oz. clear

Fragrance: 15 drops cinnamon

Molds: 2" circle mold (bar)

Other Supplies: 6 red heart soap motifs (available readymade)

Use the step-by-step instructions for the Plumaria Flowers soap as a guide. ❏

JELLY BEANS

SUPPLIES

Makes 1 soap bar.

Melt & Pour Base: 2 oz. clear soap base, 4 oz. white coconut oil soap base

Colorants: yellow, green, blue, red

Fragrance: 15 drops brown sugar

Molds: 3-3/4" x 2-1/2" domed oval (bar), jellybean candy mold (embeds)

Use the step-by-step instructions for the Plumaria Flowers soap as a guide. Make 12 jellybean soap motifs in yellow, green, blue, and red with coconut oil soap base. ❑

MINT LEAVES

SUPPLIES

Makes 1 soap bar.

Melt & Pour Base: 2 oz. clear, 4 oz. coconut oil soap base

Colorants: green

Fragrance: 10 drops spearmint

Molds: 2-1/2" domed circle (bar), leaf candy mold (embeds)

Use the step-by-step instructions for the Plumaria Flowers soap as a guide. Make 5 green leaf soap motifs with coconut oil soap base. ❑

SEA LIFE

SUPPLIES

Makes 1 soap bar.

Melt & Pour Base: 4 oz. clear soap base

Colorants: blue, green

Fragrance: 15 drops ocean

Molds: 3-3/4" x 2-1/2" domed oval (bar), sea life tray soap mold (embeds)

Use the step-by-step instructions for the Plumaria Flowers soap as a guide. Make white shells, green sea horses, and blue shell soap motifs with coconut oil soap base. ❑

Pictured clockwise from left: Sea Life, Jelly Beans, Mint Leaves.

SOAP SWIRLS

SUPPLIES

Makes 1 soap bar.

Melt & Pour Base: 4 oz. soap base (if using clear curls, then use whitened soap base, and vice versa.)

Fragrance & Colorants: your choice

Molds: individual bar-shaped molds

Other Supplies: Soap curls made by cutting soap with a soap beveller, cheese plane, or sharp knife

HERE'S HOW

1. Make a large bar of colored soap by pouring melted glycerin soap base 1" deep in a small loaf mold. Let set and release.

2. With the soap beveller held tight to the long edge of the soap bar, pull to cut a long soap curl. (photo 1)

3. Place the soap curls in the soap mold. If you curl them tight, you can fit quite a few curls in the mold. (photo 2)

Continued on next page

Soap swirls, another form of embedded soap, is a quick and easy soap technique with fun results. You can buy readymade colored soap swirls (also called "curls") or make your own from clear and/or white glycerin soap using a soap beveler, cheese plane, or knife to cut the soap. *NOTE: Because it is harder, coconut oil soap will not make successful soap curls so don't use it for this bar.*

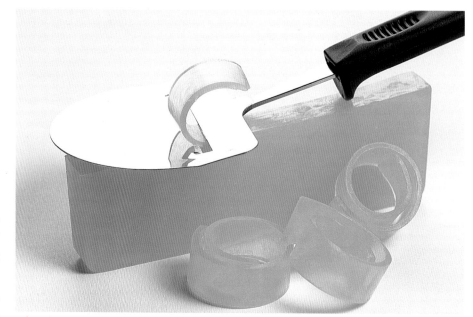

Glycerine soap being cut with a soap beveler

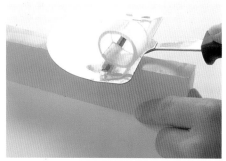

Photo 1 - Cut soap curls using a soap beveler.

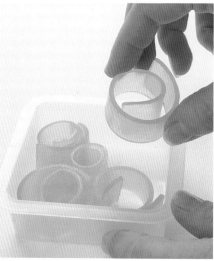

Photo 2 - Place the soap curls in the mold.

Photo 3 - Pour melted soap over the chilled soap curls.

4. Chill the mold and the soap curls in the refrigerator for 10 minutes.

5. Melt enough soap to fill the mold. Add fragrance and colorant. Pour the colored and scented soap base in around the soap curls. (photo 3) Let set and release.

6. Trim the top of the soap bar with a sharp knife or the soap beveller to revel the curled design. ❑

Embossing soaps allows you to add a design to a soap to make it more personal. In this chapter there are several types of embossing I have used to create the soaps.

"Rubber Stamp Embossing" uses rubber stamps to create a design on the soaps. Read the instructions to learn my special trick to using these rubber stamp designs. Since there are hundreds and hundreds of rubber stamps now available

Embossed Soaps

there is no limit to the look of soap you can create. You can even emboss the soap with words such as "Happy Birthday" or a loved ones name.

"Soap Stamps" are now available and make it easy to stamp a design into the soap. However, there are limited designs available.

With "Custom Embossing" you use polymer clay to make a design. When this clay design has hardened, it is placed in the bottom of the soap mold to emboss your soaps. So if you can't find a rubber stamp design you want – you can make it yourself. And it is much less expensive also.

RUBBER STAMP EMBOSSING

Rubber stamps are an excellent way to emboss a design into the surface of your soap bar – many different motifs are available. For best results, choose a stamp that is deeply etched with a clean cut around the motif. The stamp is not harmed and can be used to stamp matching paper for packaging.

SUPPLIES

Makes 1 soap bar.

Melt & Pour Base: 6 oz. coconut oil soap base

Fragrance & Color: Your choice

Mold: individual bar-shaped mold

Other Supplies:

Rubber stamps

Rubber stamp ink pad (waterproof dye inkpads work best)

Rubber cement

Photo 1 - Peel the rubber stamp from its wooden base and handle.

Photo 2 - Glue the rubber stamp in the bottom of the mold.

HERE'S HOW

1. Prepare a rubber stamp by carefully peeling the stamp from its wooden base. (photo 1) *TIP:* Place the stamp in the microwave for 20 seconds to help it come apart easily.

2. Press the stamp on a stamp pad (the ink will give the embossed image more contrast).

3. Glue the stamp, right side up, in the bottom of the mold with a small amount of rubber cement. (photo 2) NOTE: If you use too much rubber cement, it will be harder to release the soap.

4. Pour the colored and scented soap base in the mold. (photo 3)

5. When the soap has set, remove from the mold. The rubber stamp will come out with the soap.

6. Use a straight pin to help you carefully pry the stamp from the hardened soap. ❏

Photo 3 - Pour melted soap base in the mold.

Soap Stamp Embossing

SUPPLIES

Makes 1 soap bar.

Melt & Pour Base: 6 oz. coconut oil soap base

Fragrance & Color: Your choice

Mold: individual bar-shaped mold

Other Supplies:

Soap stamp

Hammer

Beautifully crafted stamps are made especially for embossing soaps. This is a much quicker method than using rubber stamps for embossing soaps if you are planning to do more than one. Be sure to stamp the soap as soon as it comes out of the mold.

HERE'S HOW

1. Pour the scented and colored soap base into the soap mold. Let set and release.

2. Set the soap on a hard, level surface. Place the stamp in the center of the soap bar. Pound the back of the soap stamp with a hammer to make the impression in the soap. (See photo.) ❏

Pictured above: A stamp for soap.

Pictured at right: Stamping a bar of soap with a soap stamp.

CUSTOM EMBOSSING SOAPS

SUPPLIES

Makes 1 soap bar.

Melt & Pour Base: 6 oz. coconut oil soap base

Fragrance & Color: Your choice

Mold: individual bar-shaped mold

Other Supplies:

Polymer clay (light color)

Wooden dowel or roller

Glazed ceramic tile, to use as a work surface

Craft knife

Rubber cement, for adhering motifs in molds

Straight pin, to help remove the motif from the soap

Optional: Pasta machine, for rolling the clay

With polymer clay, you can make your own shapes for embossing and emboss the soap using the same technique used with rubber stamps. After unmolding the soap and removing the polymer clay shapes, you can leave the soap with the embossed impression or fill it with a contrasting color of soap to create a truly unique bar. And you can use the polymer clay shapes again and again.

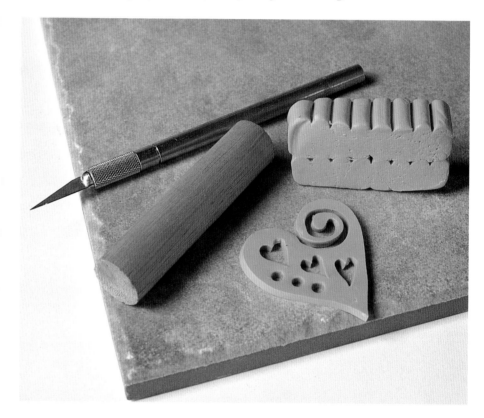

HERE'S HOW

Making the clay shape

1. Roll out the polymer clay to an even, smooth 1/8" thickness on a glazed ceramic tile. (photo 1 on page 90) (A pasta machine works extremely well for this.)

2. Trace the design on a piece of paper. Transfer the design to the clay by placing the paper pattern on the clay and lightly tracing it with a sharp pencil to make a light impression in the clay. (photo 2) *NOTE:* Lettering must be done backwards to come out right on the finished bar.

3. Holding a craft knife at a 90-degree angle to the tile, cut out the motif. (photo 3) Remove the excess polymer clay, leaving the motif on the tile.

4. Place the tile in the oven and bake the shape according to the clay manufacturer's directions. Let cool.

Continued on page 90

Pictured right, clockwise from top: Love, Peace Flower, Embossed Hearts

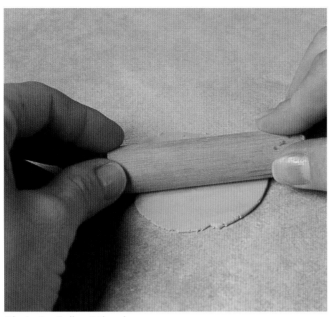

Photo 1 - Roll out the clay.

Continued from page 88

Molding the soap

1. Glue the polymer clay shape to the bottom of the mold with a small amount of rubber cement. (photo 4)

2. Pour in the scented, colored soap base. Let set. Release. (The polymer clay shapes will come out of the mold with the soap.)

3. Use a straight pin to help you, carefully pry the motif from the hardened soap.

*Option: **Adding a second color***

1. Place the soap bar in the refrigerator to chill for 10 minutes.

2. Melt a small amount of soap of a different color and pour it in the embossed depression in the soap. (Don't worry if it overfills slightly.) Let cool.

3. Using a sharp knife, trim or scrap unwanted soap away to reveal the motif. ❏

Photo 2 - Transfer the design to the clay.

Photo 3 - Cut out the motif.

90

Photo 4 - Glue the baked and cooled motif in the mold.

Photo 5 - Pour melted soap base into mold.

Photo 6 - Various motifs for embossing made from polymer clay.

LOVE

Pictured on page 89

SUPPLIES

Makes one bar.

Melt & Pour Base: 4 oz. white coconut oil soap base, 1 oz. bright pink pre-colored soap base

Fragrances: 5 drops patchouli, 10 drops rose

Mold: 3-1/4" x 2" rectangle

Other Supplies: Polymer clay motifs - the letters to spell "LOVE"

HERE'S HOW

See the step-by-step instructions for Custom Embossed Soaps and follow these instructions:

1. Make the polymer clay shapes.

2. Glue in mold.

3. Melt the white coconut oil soap base. Add fragrances. Pour in mold.

4. Let set. Unmold. Remove polymer clay pieces.

5. Melt pink soap base. Pour in the embossed depressions in the soap. Let cool.

6. Trim soap. ❑

PEACE FLOWER

Pictured on page 89

SUPPLIES

Makes one bar.

Melt & Pour Base: 3 oz. white coconut oil soap base, 1 oz. bright pink pre-colored soap base

Fragrances: 5 drops patchouli, 10 drops ylang-ylang

Molds: 2-1/2" circle

Other Supplies: Polymer clay motif - peace flower

HERE'S HOW

See the step-by-step instructions for Custom Embossed Soaps and follow these instructions:

1. Make the polymer clay shape.

2. Glue in mold.

3. Melt the white coconut oil soap base. Add fragrances. Pour in mold.

4. Let set. Unmold. Remove polymer clay pieces.

5. Melt pink soap base. Pour in the embossed depressions in the soap. Let cool.

6. Trim soap. ❑

EMBOSSED HEARTS

Pictured on page 89

SUPPLIES

Makes one bar.

Melt & Pour Base: 5 oz. white coconut oil soap base, 1 oz. bright pink pre-colored soap base

Fragrances: 5 drops patchouli, 10 drops rose

Mold: 3" square

Other Supplies: Polymer clay motif, heart

HERE'S HOW

See the step-by-step instructions for Custom Embossed Soaps and follow these instructions:

1. Make the polymer clay shape.

2. Glue in mold.

3. Melt the white coconut oil soap base. Add fragrances. Pour in mold.

4. Let set. Unmold. Remove polymer clay pieces.

5. Melt pink soap base. Pour in the embossed depressions in the soap. Let cool.

6. Trim soap. ❏

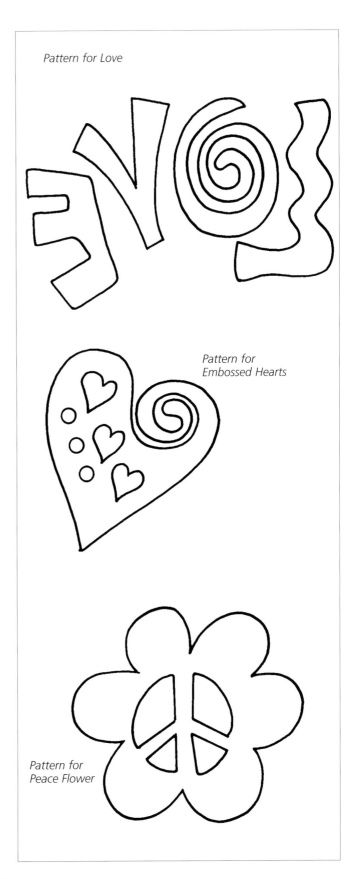

Pattern for Love

Pattern for
Embossed Hearts

Pattern for
Peace Flower

FLEUR DE LIS

SUPPLIES

Makes one bar.

Melt & Pour Base: 6 oz. clear glycerin soap base

Colorants: 1/4 teaspoon gold luster powder, 1 drop black, 2 drops orange

Fragrances: 15 drops violet, 5 drops amber

Additive: pinch of dried peppermint leaves

Mold: 3" oval

Other Supplies: Polymer clay motif - fleur de lis

HERE'S HOW

See the step-by-step instructions for Custom Embossed Soaps and follow these instructions:

1. Make the polymer clay shape.

2. Glue in mold.

3. Melt 5 oz. clear glycerin soap base. Add fragrances and gold luster powder. Pour in mold.

4. Let set. Unmold. Remove polymer clay piece.

5. Melt remaining 1 oz. clear soap base. Add a pinch of dried peppermint leaves and 1 drop black and two drops orange colorants to make a clear auburn hue. Pour in the embossed depression in the soap. Let cool.

6. Trim soap if necessary to clean up. ❏

Pattern for Fleur de lis

SPEARMINT LEAVES

SUPPLIES

Makes one bar.

Melt & Pour Base: 5 oz. white coconut oil soap base, 1 oz. clear glycerin soap base

Colorants: 5 drops green

Fragrance: 15 drops spearmint

Additive: 1/2 teaspoon dried peppermint leaves

Mold: 3" oval

Other Supplies: Polymer clay motif - leaf sprig

HERE'S HOW

See the step-by-step instructions for Custom Embossed Soaps and follow these instructions:

1. Make the polymer clay shape.

2. Glue in mold.

3. Melt white coconut oil soap base. Add fragrance, 4 drops green colorant, and dried peppermint leaves. Pour in mold.

4. Let set. Unmold. Remove polymer clay piece.

5. Melt clear glycerin soap base. Add 1 drop green colorant. Pour in the embossed depression in the soap. Let cool.

6. Trim soap if necessary. ❏

Pattern for Spearmint Leaves

FOSSIL SOAPS

Instructions follow on page 98

SUPPLIES

Makes one bar.

Melt & Pour Base: 6 oz. coconut oil soap base

Fragrance & Color: your choice

Mold: individual bar-shaped mold

Other Supplies:

Heavy duty aluminum foil

Plastic toy fish, bugs, lizards, or dinosaurs

Sharp knife

Rubber cement

Pinch of paprika as additive

These soaps are easy and fun to make with children. The plastic toy animals leave detailed impressions in the finished soap.

Lining the mold with aluminum foil gives a natural stone look to the finished soap. Adding a pinch of paprika, which sinks to the bottom when you pour the hot melted soap base, gives more color contrast and a more natural appearance.

Instructions follow on page 98

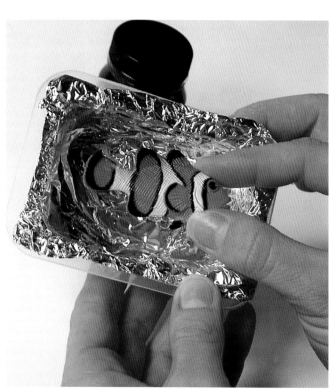

Photo 1 - Glue the plastic animal (here, a toy fish) in the mold.

Photo 2 - Add a pinch of paprika to the mold.

HERE'S HOW

1. Line the mold with aluminum foil.

2. Glue the plastic toy face up in the bottom of the mold with rubber cement. (photo 1) *NOTE:* If you don't glue it, it will float to the top.

3. Melt the soap base. Add a pinch of paprika to the mold. (photo 2) Pour the hot soap in the mold. Let set and release.

4. Use a knife to carve out the plastic toy from the soap. ❑

PREHISTORIC FISH

SUPPLIES

Makes one bar.

Melt & Pour Base: 2-1/2 to 5 oz. white glycerin soap base

Colorants: 2 drops green, 2 drops blue (for teal); 3 drops green, 1 drop red (for moss green)

Fragrance: 5 drops ginger, 5 drops melon

Additive: 1/4 teaspoon paprika per bar

Molds: individual bar-shaped mold

Other Supplies: plastic toy fish

Line mold with foil and follow step-by-step instructions for Fossil Soaps. ❑

CAVE MAN

SUPPLIES

Makes one bar.

Melt & Pour Base: 4 oz. coconut oil soap base

Fragrance: 10 drops earth

Colorant: 5 drops sand color

Additive: 1/2 teaspoon dried bergamot leaves

Mold: 4-oz. rectangle lined with aluminum foil

Other Supplies: Stencil with prehistoric people motifs, soap paint

Line mold with foil and mold soap. Stencil on the prehistoric design with soap paint. ❑

PREHISTORIC BEETLE

SUPPLIES

Makes one bar.

Melt & Pour Base: 3 oz. whitened glycerin soap base

Colorants: 5 drops red, 3 drops black

Fragrance: 10 drops amber

Additive: 1/4 teaspoon dried peppermint leaves

Mold: 2-3/4" x 2" small rectangle

Other Supplies: Plastic toy beetle, heavy duty aluminum foil

Line mold with foil and follow step-by-step instructions for Fossil Soaps. ❑

Pictured right, beginning top center moving clockwise: Prehistoric Fish, Centipede Fossil, Prehistoric Beetle, Cave Man.

CENTIPEDE FOSSIL

Pictured on page 99

The plastic toy centipede placed on the bottom of the mold creates the fossil. Makes one bar.

SUPPLIES

Melt & Pour Base: 5 oz. coconut oil soap base

Fragrance: 10 drops chocolate

Colorant: 5 drops sand

Additive: 1 teaspoon poppy seeds

Mold: 5-oz. square mold lined with aluminum foil

Other Supplies: Plastic toy centipede, aluminum foil

Line mold with foil and follow step-by-step instructions for Fossil Soaps. ❏

DINOSAUR EGGS

Pictured on page 101

The egg soaps with the lizards hatching combine fossil soap and carved soap techniques. The little lizard remains in the soap rather than leaving an impression. This makes 3 bars – if you have 3 oval molds, you can make them all at once.

SUPPLIES

Makes on bar.

Melt & Pour Base: 8 oz. clear glycerin soap base

Colorants: 8 drops orange, 4 drops black (to make brown)

Fragrance: 20 drops amber

Mold: 2" x 3" x 3/4" deep

Other Supplies: 3 small plastic lizards, rubber cement

HERE'S HOW

1. Glue the plastic toy face up in the bottom of the mold with rubber cement.

2. Melt the soap base. Add colorants and fragrance. Pour the hot soap in the mold. Let set and release.

3. Use a knife to carve away part of the oval to make the egg. ❏

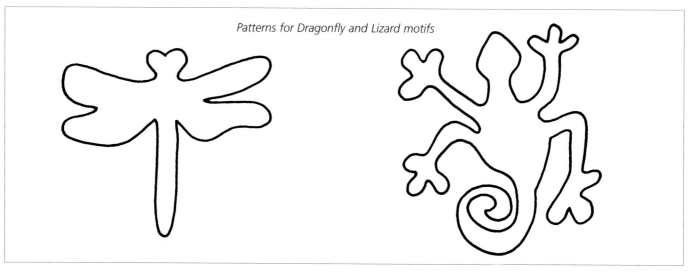

Patterns for Dragonfly and Lizard motifs

Pictured clockwise beginning at top left: Dragonfly Soap, Lizard Soap, Dinosaur Eggs.

The Dragonfly and Lizard soaps use polymer clay motifs to make the embossed image in the soap, and a second color is added in the impression left by the "fossil." See the section on Custom Embossed Soaps and follow the instructions for the "Adding a Second Color" option in that section.

101

Carved Soaps

Carving is an easy, fun way to accent a soap bar. You can use a small sharp knife (one without serrated edges) to carve out a design or whittle the soap into a new shape. A woodcarving set with V-shaped gouges is useful for carving designs and letters on soap bars.

In designing the carved bars, I wanted to take away only a small amount of soap to create the design. I used two different carving techniques, relief carving and two-toned carving.

RELIEF CARVING

Relief carving etches a simple design in the top of the soap for maximal effect with minimal effort. I like to carve words to make messages on soaps – like "joy," "comfort," and "dream." You could also carve someone's name on a soap bar for a special gift.

SUPPLIES

Soap bar

Small sharp knife

Carving tool with 3/16" narrow V-shaped gouge

Pattern

Terrycloth

HERE'S HOW

1. Melt the soap bases. Add colorant(s) and fragrance(s). Make a marbled bar of soap by pouring white soap and colored soap in the mold at the same time.

2. Pour in mold. Let set and release.

3. Trace pattern on a piece of paper. Place the pattern on the bar of soap and trace over the lines with a pen. The pressure of the pen leaves a faint impression for you to follow when you carve. (photo 1)

4. Using the tip of a sharp knife or a V-shaped gouging tool, carve the design. Go slowly to prevent slipping. (photo 2)

5. Deepen the carving a little at a time by going over the carved line until you are satisfied with the result. The deeper you go, the greater the color change in the marbled bar.

6. Polish by lightly wiping with a piece of terrycloth. ❏

Photo 1 - Trace the pattern on the soap.

Photo 2 - Carve the soap with a carving tool.

COMFORT

Pictured on page 102

SUPPLIES

Makes one bar.

Melt & Pour Base: 3 oz. whitened glycerin soap base

Colorants: 2 drops red, 6 drops orange (to make coral)

Fragrances: 10 drops vanilla, 5 drops jasmine

Mold: 2" x 3" oval

Other Supplies: carving tools, "Comfort" lettering pattern, terrycloth

Follow the step-by-step instructions for Relief Carving. ❏

JOY

Pictured on page 102

SUPPLIES

Makes one bar.

Melt & Pour Base: 3 oz. whitened glycerin soap base

Colorants: 6 drops yellow

Fragrance: 10 drops vanilla, 5 drops sweet orange

Mold: 2-1/2" circle

Other Supplies: carving tools, "Joy" lettering pattern, terrycloth

Follow the step-by-step instructions for Relief Carving. ❏

Patterns are found on page 107

RELAX

Pictured on page 102

SUPPLIES

Makes one bar.

Melt & Pour Base: 3 oz. whitened glycerin soap base

Colorant: 4 drops green

Fragrance: 10 drops lavender, 6 drops ylang-ylang

Mold: 2" x 3" oval

Other Supplies: carving tools, "Relax" lettering pattern, terrycloth

Follow the step-by-step instructions for Relief Carving. ❏

DREAM

Pictured on page 102

SUPPLIES

Makes one bar.

Melt & Pour Base: 4 oz. whitened glycerin soap base

Colorants: 6 drops blue, 2 drops orange

Fragrances: 10 drops chamomile, 5 drops lavender

Mold: 3-1/4" x 2-1/4" rectangle

Other Supplies: carving supplies, "Dream" lettering pattern, terrycloth

Follow the step-by-step instructions for Relief Carving. ❏

PEACE

Pictured on page 102

SUPPLIES

Makes one bar.

Melt & Pour Base: 3 oz. whitened glycerin soap base

Colorant: 6 drops blue

Fragrances: 10 drops vanilla, 5 drops sandalwood

Mold: 2-1/2" circle

Other Supplies: carving tools, "Peace" lettering pattern, terrycloth

Follow the step-by-step instructions for Relief Carving. ❏

UPLIFT

Pictured on page 102

SUPPLIES

Makes one bar.

Melt & Pour Base: 4 oz. whitened glycerin soap base

Colorant: 5 drops red

Fragrances: 10 drops sweet orange, 5 drops peppermint

Mold: 3-1/4" x 2-1/4" rectangle

Other Supplies: carving supplies, "Uplift" lettering pattern, terrycloth

Follow the step-by-step instructions for Relief Carving. ❏

Patterns for Relief Carving on Soaps

Joy

Peace

Relax

Comfort

Dream

Uplift

TWO-TONED CARVING

SUPPLIES

Small sharp knife

Carving tool with 3/16" narrow V-shaped gouge

Pattern

Terrycloth

Plastic cup

Wax paper

Two-toned carving is a little more complicated. Before you carve, you must first make a two-toned bar of soap.

The best way I've found to make two-toned bars for carving is to pour a contrasting color of soap over a molded bar – this creates wonderful contrast as you carve the details. I experimented with pouring colored layers in a mold, but those soaps were not as successful as pouring the different color over the soap bar. You need only a thin layer of color so you don't have to carve too deeply. Use a piece of terrycloth for polishing and smoothing the carved design. *TIP:* Carve over a wax paper covered area and reclaim the carvings to melt again for future soapmaking.

The Two-Toned Daisy illustrates the two-toned carving technique. Specific instructions follow.

Photo 1 - The soap bar (on an upturned plastic cup) covered with the contrasting color.

Photo 2 - Trace the pattern on the soap bar.

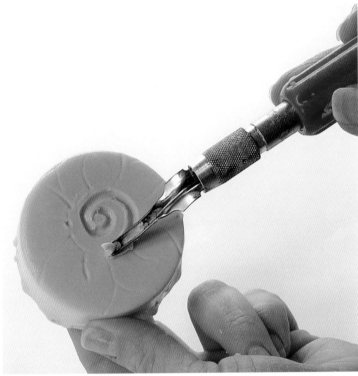

Photo 3 - Carve the soap with a gouging tool to reveal the second color.

HERE'S HOW

Creating a two-toned bar

1. Melt enough soap base to fill your chosen mold. Add colorant(s) and fragrance(s). Pour the scented and colored soap into the mold. Let set. Release.

2. Cover your work area with wax paper. Place the molded bar on an upturned plastic cup. Pour 2 oz. of melted soap in a contrasting color over the bar. (photo 1) Let the soap set. Repeat, if needed. Reclaim the soap dribbles on the wax paper to use again. *TIP:* You will get thicker coverage if the melted soap is cooled slightly by stirring.

Carving

1. Trace the pattern you wish to carve on a piece of paper. Place the pattern on top of the bar and trace with a pen. (photo 2) The pressure of the pen will leave a faint impression on the bar to guide you.

2. Divide the bar in half horizontally by marking a line around the sides of the bar.

3. Using the tip of a sharp knife or a V-shaped gouge carving tool, slowly (so the tool doesn't slip) carve the design, following the guidelines. Carve down to the scored mark on the side of the soap. (photo 3)

4. Carve below the scored mark to form petals below the first ones. (They will be a different color, creating the two-toned effect.) (photo 4)

5. Polish the bar by lightly wiping with a piece of terrycloth. ❑

Photo 4 – Carve to form petals.

TWO-TONED DAISY

SUPPLIES

Makes one bar.

Melt & Pour Base: 5 oz. whitened glycerin soap base

Colorants: 6 drops yellow, 3 drops red

Fragrances: 10 drops jasmine, 5 drops honey

Mold: 2-1/2" circle

Other Supplies: carving tools, daisy pattern, terrycloth

HERE'S HOW

See "Two-Toned Carving" and follow these instructions:

1. Melt 3 oz. white soap base. Add fragrances and 6 drops yellow colorant. Pour in round mold. Let set. Release.

2. Melt 2 oz. white soap base. Add 3 drops red colorant for a light pink hue. Pour over yellow soap bar. Let set. Repeat, if necessary.

3. Transfer the daisy pattern to the soap. Divide the bar in half horizontally by marking a line around the sides of the bar.

4. Carve the design, following the guidelines. Carve down to the scored mark on the side of the soap.

5. Carve below the scored mark to form petals below the first ones. (They will be a different color, creating the two-toned effect.)

6. Polish with a piece of terrycloth. ❏

TWO-TONED LILAC

SUPPLIES

Makes one bar.

Melt & Pour Base: 5 oz. whitened glycerin soap base

Colorants: 4 drops green, 4 drops red, 3 drops blue

Fragrance: 10 drops lilac

Mold: 3" x 2" oval

Other Supplies: carving tools, lilac pattern, terrycloth

HERE'S HOW

See "Two-Toned Carving" and follow these instructions:

1. Melt 3 oz. white soap base. Add fragrance and 4 drops green colorant. Pour in oval mold. Let set. Release.

2. Melt 2 oz. white soap base. Add 4 drops red colorant and 3 drops blue for a purple hue. Pour over green soap bar. Let set. Repeat, if necessary.

3. Transfer the lilac pattern to the soap. Divide the bar in half horizontally by marking a line around the sides of the bar.

4. Carve the design, following the guidelines. Carve down to the scored mark on the side of the soap.

5. Carve below the scored mark to form petals below the first ones. (They will be a different color, creating the two-toned effect.)

6. Polish with a piece of terrycloth. ❏

TWO-TONED ROSE

Pictured on page 111

SUPPLIES

Makes one bar.

Melt & Pour Base: 7 oz. whitened glycerin soap base

Colorants: 9 drops red

Fragrances: 10 drops rose, 4 drops honey

Mold: 3" square

Other Supplies: carving tools, rose pattern, terrycloth

HERE'S HOW

See "Two-Toned Carving" and follow these instructions:

1. Melt 5 oz. white soap base. Add fragrances and 3 drops red colorant for a light pink hue. Pour in square mold. Let set. Release.

2. Melt 2 oz. white soap base. Add 6 drops red colorant for a dark pink hue. Pour over light pink soap bar. Let set. Repeat, if necessary.

3. Transfer the rose pattern to the soap. Divide the bar in half horizontally by marking a line around the sides of the bar.

4. Carve the design, following the guidelines. Carve down to the scored mark on the side of the soap.

5. Carve below the scored mark to form petals below the first ones. (They will be a different color, creating the two-toned effect.)

6. Polish with a piece of terrycloth. ❏

TWO-TONED PANSY

Pictured on page 111

SUPPLIES

Makes one bar.

Melt & Pour Base: 5 oz. whitened glycerin soap base

Colorants: 10 drops red, 3 drops blue

Fragrances: 10 drops lily of the valley, 5 drops violet

Mold: 2-1/2" circle

Other Supplies: carving tools, pansy pattern, terrycloth

HERE'S HOW

See "Two-Toned Carving" and follow these instructions:

1. Melt 3 oz. white soap base. Add fragrances and 6 drops red colorant for a dark pink hue. Pour in circle mold. Let set. Release.

2. Melt 2 oz. white soap base. Add 4 drops red colorant and 3 drops blue for a purple hue. Pour over pink soap bar. Let set. Repeat, if necessary.

3. Transfer the pansy pattern to the soap.

4. Carve the design, following the guidelines and the photo.

5. Carve the lower petal as shown. (It is a different color, creating the two-toned effect.)

6. Polish with a piece of terrycloth. ❏

Patterns for Carved Flower Soaps

Daisy

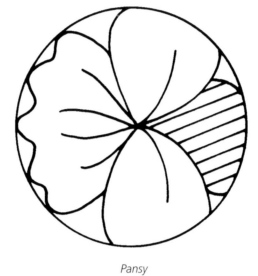

Pansy

Rose

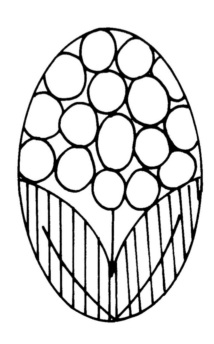

Lilac

Small Creative Soaps

Small tube molds make creating small soaps quick and uncomplicated. The soaps in this section are great for using up all the little leftover pieces of colored soap from other projects. You'll also see fun and quirky ideas for presenting and packaging small soaps.

SOAP BOUQUET

Pictured on page 114

SUPPLIES

Melt & Pour Base: leftover scraps of clear and white soap bases

Colorants: flower colors, and yellow for centers

Fragrances: assorted floral scents

Molds: 1-1/2" flower shaped tube, 1-1/2" heart tube

Other Supplies:

Bamboo skewers

Light green acrylic craft paint

Paint brush

Green-colored bath salts made with chunky sea salt

Clay pot

Clear cellophane

Thin ribbon

HERE'S HOW

1. Pour the colored, fragrant soap base in prepared molds. Follow the instructions for Oval Floral soap for making a flower with a different-colored center. Let set and release.

2. Paint the bamboo skewers with green acrylic craft paint. Let dry.

3. Cut the heart in half lengthwise to create the green leaves. (photo 1)

4. Cut the blossoms and the leaves into 1" thick slices. (photo 2)

5. Carefully pierce the soaps with bamboo skewers. (photo 3)

6. Cover the blossom and leaves with a 12" square of cellophane and tie with a matching ribbon at the base.

7. For presentation of the bouquet soaps, push the speared soaps into a clay pot filled with fragrant bath salts. ❑

Photo 1 - Cut the green heart tube in half to form the leaves.

Photo 2 - Slice the soaps.

Photo 3 - Place the soaps on the bamboo skewer "stems."

SOAP BEADS

SUPPLIES

Melt & Pour Base: leftover scraps of clear and white soap bases

Colorants: yellow, blue, red

Fragrances: assorted floral scents

Molds: 1" circle tube, 1-1/2" heart tube, 1-1/2" star tube

Other Supplies: large-eye needle, 1/8" wide ribbon

HERE'S HOW

1. Pour the colored, fragrant soap base in prepared tube molds. Let set. Release.

2. Cut into 1/2" to 1" thick slices.

3. Thread ribbon through a large-eye needle. String the soap beads on the ribbon. Knot both ends of the ribbon so the soap won't fall off. ❑

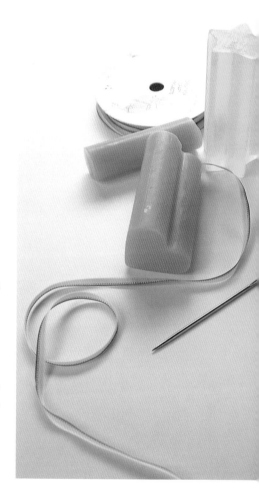

▓ Floral Soap Beads

Use a 1-1/2" blossom tube mold. Follow the instructions for Oval Floral soap for making a flower with a different-colored center.

Pictured at right: Cocktail Soaps. Instructions follow on next page.

COCKTAIL SOAPS

Pictured on page 119

These small soaps-on-a-skewer are easy to make. Use them as part of a gift basket or party favors.

SUPPLIES

Melt & Pour Base: clear glycerin soap base

Colorants: green, red

Fragrances: lemon, lime, cucumber, juniper

Molds: 1" circle tube mold, 1-1/2" blossom tube mold

Other Supplies: plastic straw, bamboo skewers, clear cellophane, thin green ribbon, garnish knife with wavy pattern

HERE'S HOW

1. Pour the colored, fragrant soap base in the prepared molds.

   Olive: See the Martini soap instructions for creating the olive.

   Onion: Pour clear soap into the 1" tube mold for the onion. *Pickle:* Pour clear soap with green colorant in the 1-1/2" small blossom tube mold for the sweet pickle slice.

   Let set and release.

2. Cut the olive and onion soaps into 3/4" thick slices. Cut the green blossom soap column 3/4" thick with a garnish knife to create the sweet pickle.

3. Carefully pierce the soaps with bamboo skewers.

4. Cover with a 12" square of cellophane. Tie with ribbon at the base. ❏

SOAPSICLES

Pictured on page 121

These look and smell good enough to eat, so be sure to label them as soap.

SUPPLIES

Melt & Pour Base: coconut oil soap base

Colorants: red, orange, black

Fragrance: vanilla, raspberry vanilla, chocolate

Molds: 2-3/4" x 2" rectangle, 1-1/2" x 1" rectangle

Other Supplies: small cellophane bags, craft sticks, plastic cups, wax paper, natural raffia

HERE'S HOW

1. In two containers, melt enough soap base to make the bars. Tint the soap in one container with a few drops of pink colorant to make a pink hue. Scent the white soap with vanilla. Scent the pink soap with raspberry vanilla.

2. Pour the melted and scented soap into the rectangle molds. Let set and release.

3. Melt 2 oz. of soap base and add enough orange and black colorants to make a dark brown. Scent with chocolate fragrance oil. *TIP:* You will get thicker coverage if you cool the soap slightly by stirring.

4. Cover your work area with wax paper. Place one bar on an upturned plastic cup and pour the "chocolate" coating over the bar. Repeat, if necessary. Let set. Reclaim the soap on the wax paper and use again.

5. When the "chocolate" coating is complete, carefully push a wooden craft stick in the bottom of the soap bar. *Option:* For a whimsical presentation, carve a "bite" out of the top of your soapsicle.

6. Cover with a small cellophane bag and tie with a piece of natural raffia at the base. ❏

TUB TREATS

These little soaps that look like candies are created in small tube molds or small individual molds with a variety of techniques. When designing soap sweets, keep the colors coordinated and use yummy-scented fragrance oils. Have fun creating different designs, and be sure to label the Tub Treats as soap so no one mistakes them for edibles!

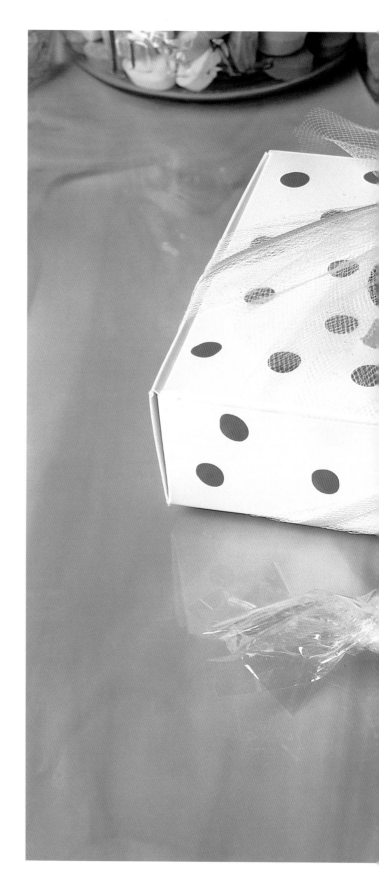

SUPPLIES

Melt & Pour Base: your choice – this is a good way to use small amounts of leftover soap base

Colorants: your choice – here, I used red, blue, green

Fragrances: your choice – try brown sugar, candy cane, cinnamon, honey, almond, or vanilla

Molds: small tube molds or small individual bar molds

Other Supplies: straws, soap beveller, clear cellophane, clear tape, white candy box painted with colored dots and a gold seal *or* cellophane bag and ribbon

HERE'S HOW

Creating the soaps

• *Polka-dot soap* - Use plastic straws and a small circle tube mold. Cut into slices 3/4" thick.

• *Layered soap* - Pour layers of color in a small rectangle mold. Trim with a soap beveller.

• Blossom shaped soap - Place chunks of colored soap in a prepared 1-1/2" blossom tube mold. Chill. Pour in a contrasting color. Cut into slices 3/4" thick.

Packaging

1. Cut cellophane into 6" squares. Wrap soaps and twist ends. *TIP:* Use clear tape at the back for an invisible closure before twisting the ends tightly.

2. Place in a cellophane bag or a candy box. ❑

SOAP GEMS

SUPPLIES

Melt & Pour Base: leftover scraps of colored, scented soap – enough to fill a 3" square mold

Fragrance: a blending fragrance, such as vanilla, honey, or lavender

Mold: 3" square

Other Supplies: sheer fabric bag

HERE'S HOW

1. Sort soap scraps into complementary color groups.

2. Cut some of the soap scraps into chunks. Place the chunks in a 3" square mold. Refrigerate for 10 minutes.

3. Melt remaining soap scraps. Add fragrance. Stir to cool. Pour in mold.

4. Let set. Release.

5. Cut the bar into large, irregular pieces to form the gems. Trim the edges to form the facets.

6. Package in a sheer fabric bag. ❑

Pictured at right: Three-Dimensional Soaps. Instructions follow on page 126.

THREE-DIMENSIONAL SOAPS

Small decorative soaps are attached to larger bars for accent. You can adhere the decorative soaps with clear melted soap or present them placed on top of the large bars, packaged together. The pairings provide a small fancy soap for the sink soap dish and a large bar for the shower or tub.

The smaller soaps use decorative tray molds. To make the small soaps with defined color areas, you will have to do two moldings. For example if you are making a lemon with green leaves, first pour yellow soap base in a lemon-shaped mold. After releasing the soap, trim off the leaves and place the molded lemon piece back in the mold. After chilling the piece, pour in green soap base so the leaves would be green. See an assortment of these soaps pictured on page 125.

RASPBERRY CREAM

SUPPLIES

This recipe is courtesy Environmental Technologies. It makes one bar set.

Melt & Pour Base: 5 oz. whitened glycerin soap base

Fragrance: 10 drops raspberry vanilla

Colorants: 1 drop red (for base of raspberry), 1 drop green (for raspberry leaves), 3 drops red (for oval bar)

Molds: 3 oz. oval (for bar), grape cluster tray mold (for the raspberry)

Mold as described previously. ❏

HONEYSUCKLE BLOSSOM

SUPPLIES

This recipe is courtesy Environmental Technologies. It makes two bar sets.

Melt & Pour Base: 7 oz. whitened glycerin soap base

Fragrance: 10 drops honeysuckle

Colorant: 3 drops yellow to 2 oz. soap base (for blossoms)

Molds: 3 oz. round mold (for bar), small blossoms motif in tray mold

Mold as described previously. ❏

CHERUBS

SUPPLIES

Makes two bar sets.

Melt & Pour Base: 8 oz. whitened glycerin soap base

Fragrances 10 drops baby powder, 5 drops lily of the valley

Colorants: 2 drops red, 1 drop blue to 2 oz. soap base (for cherubs), 3 drops red to 6 oz. soap base (for rectangle bar)

Additive: Pinch of iridescent powder (for cherubs)

Molds: Small cherub tray mold, 3 oz. rectangle (for bar)

Mold as described previously. ❏

FRUIT

SUPPLIES

Makes one bar set.

Melt & Pour Bases: 2 oz. clear glycerin soap base (for fruit), 5 oz. whitened glycerin soap base (for square bar)

Fragrances: 5 drops mango, 10 drops melon

Colorants: Red (for strawberry), purple (for grapes), yellow (for banana), orange (for pear), 3 drops green (for the bar)

Molds: Tray of fruit motifs, 5-oz. square (for bar)

Other Supplies: Green soap paint

Mold as described previously. Accent the fruit with a little green paint. ❏

METRIC CONVERSION CHART
INCHES TO MILLIMETERS AND CENTIMETERS

Inches	MM	CM		Yards	Meters
1/8	3	.3		1/8	.11
1/4	6	.6		1/4	.23
3/8	10	1.0		3/8	.34
1/2	13	1.3		1/2	.46
5/8	16	1.6		5/8	.57
3/4	19	1.9		3/4	.69
7/8	22	2.2		7/8	.80
1	25	2.5		1	.91
1-1/4	32	3.2		2	1.83
1-1/2	38	3.8		3	2.74
1-3/4	44	4.4		4	3.66
2	51	5.1		5	4.57
3	76	7.6		6	5.49
4	102	10.2		7	6.40
5	127	12.7		8	7.32
6	152	15.2		9	8.23
7	178	17.8		10	9.14
8	203	20.3			
9	229	22.9			
10	254	25.4			
11	279	27.9			
12	305	30.5			

INDEX